Becoming Dungeon Master

An Instruction Manual for the Game We're All Playing

KENTON WHITMAN

ReWild University Press

Some names and identifying details of people described in this book have been altered to protect their privacy.

ISBN: 978-1-7377378-1-0
Cover design by Rebecca Whitman
Illustrations by Mirabelle Whitman

To Rebecca, Mirabelle, and Liliana, my fellow adventurers through life's mysteries.

Becoming Dungeon Master

satori instruction manual contents

Preface

As children we are educated about our world. But we're usually taught only about the most obvious aspects of the world, the "consensus reality" that makes up our current cultural paradigm. Few of us are taught one of the greatest secrets of life, which is that our foundational beliefs about reality have a profound effect on the world we experience.

This is true for both individuals and for humanity as a whole. Do you believe the world is essentially evil? If so, you will largely experience an evil world. Do you think the world is utterly mysterious and fascinating? If so, you will see fascinating mysteries everywhere you look. It's like the anecdote of the mycologist and entomologist who went for a hike together. At the end of the hike, the entomologist said, "Wow, did you see all those insects?" And the mycologist says, "Insects? The only bugs I saw were those nasty mosquitoes. But there were tons of mushrooms!"

We all know that two people can look at the same experience and have vastly different interpretations (licorice is justifiably famous for being delicious to one person and disgusting to the next). Anyone who has paid attention to their own life has noticed this in themselves as well — we can interpret any situation in a way that makes it positive or a way that makes it negative.

But this "foundation of reality" goes deeper than simply liking things or disliking things. It creates our basic *sensation* of life, of what life *feels* like.

Most of us have been given a mechanistic foundation of the world, and as a result, we see the world as composed of chopped-up bits that ideally would fit together nicely but in reality seem to always be falling apart. Because of this viewpoint, we spend most of our life energies trying to make the pieces of life fit together. For many, this equates with working a job we don't like so we can pay all the bills waiting for us each month, or trying to maintain family or friend relationships so they don't become disasters, or battling our own inner demons that keep us embroiled in habits we wish we could break.

Relatively few of us wake up each morning and look forward to a day of adventure, creativity, exciting challenges, and fun.

But is a life of trying to keep things from falling apart really the way life is? Is it "real life", "hard reality"? Or is it just the product of a certain way of viewing the world?

Some visionary scientists are beginning to see outside the constraints of modern thought. Rizwan Virk in *The Simulation Hypothesis,* Amit Goswami in *The Self-Aware Universe,* and Robert Lanza and Bob Berman in *Biocentrism* all offer up elegant new ways to frame the universe that could revolutionize our thoughts, assumptions, actions, and even our basic sensation of life. This book doesn't claim to offer a new scientific hypothesis, which is already accomplished by those aforementioned authors. Rather, it offers an alternative "everyday" way of encountering the world.

By the end of this book, you'll come to find that "real life" may not be what you've been taught to believe. You'll not only recognize that your foundational beliefs about life dictate the world you experience, but you'll have learned how to transform those beliefs. As you do, you'll find that the world you experience begins to shift. At first the change will be slow, but as it gains momentum and you become more familiar with influencing that change, you'll start to wake up each morning looking forward to a day of adventure, creativity, exciting challenges, and fun.

It isn't easy to change our basic viewpoints of reality. These things are given to us by the scientific models, religions, and dominant cultural trends of our times.

We've grown up steeped in these things so that they've infused every corner of our minds. What we need is a new perception that will take the world we're already experiencing, the beliefs we already hold, and reframe them so they not only make more sense, but so they *feel* right.

This book will give you that new perception, and it does so in the spirit of play and myth. Get ready for the adventure of a lifetime, because you are holding the instruction manual for the most amazing game imaginable —

Satori, the game we're all playing.

introduction

My wife Rebecca and I have lived an adventure-filled life. We've been horse trainers, SCUBA divers, and the Directors of Entertainment for a Renaissance faire. We've run a belly dance troupe, trained street actors, taught martial arts, tracked wolves for the Wisconsin DNR, helped addicts overcome their addictions, and been ghost-hunters. In recent years we ran ReWild University, a unique wilderness school where people came from around the world to live for up to a year in the forest, training in martial arts, survival skills, and meditation.

During all of this time, we've been gaming.

We began dice-and-paper gaming early in our relationship. At first it was AD&D, but then we discovered an obscure system called Dragonquest. Over time, we started "bending the rules" to make Dragonquest more fun, and eventually we created our own world and system. We even designed a website to share our world and role-playing game, and to detail the creatures, lands, and peoples that made up our world of Carador (now archived on the Wayback Machine when you search caradorian.com).

We loved role-playing so much that we wanted to play everywhere – when driving, when working (we worked together at the time as housekeeping inspectors at a resort in Colorado), when eating at a restaurant. But the looks we got when rolling our dice on the table at the local pizza parlor made us feel a bit awkward. Eventually, we phased out the dice.

I know. This might sound like heresy. Dice, and the randomness they bring to a game, are at the heart of what makes a role-playing game a role-playing game. They can steer the game in new directions, and give us those glorious moments when we make a perfect roll and slay the dragon with a single arrow (or those heart-rending moments when our character of the past three years is taken down by the dragon).

Something was lost when we gave up the dice. But something was also gained. Now we could bring our game anywhere, because all we needed was each other. And the Dungeon Master gained a new responsibility and new power, to "roll the dice in one's head". This allowed the DM to sculpt stories in a new way, because the DM was no longer beholden to the dice. In effect, our role-playing experience was a slow transition from accepting someone else's universe to creating our own, where we made the rules. This could also be seen as a transition from an atheistic universe, guided by overarching rules and the randomness of the dice, to a more spiritual and participatory universe, guided solely by the creativity of the DM.

This last point is important, because at the same time that we were experimenting with role-playing, we were experimenting with spirituality. Rebecca grew up Christian, and I grew up atheist. Both of us were fed up with our original viewpoints, Rebecca because she saw the hypocrisy of the church, and I because my initial investigations into Zen and other Eastern thought-systems showed me that the modern scientific world-view was still belief-based. It assumed as fact some things such as subject-object duality and the primacy of matter, and justified those assumptions using Occam's razor. Occam's razor might hold a certain appeal, but it doesn't rescue the scientific viewpoint from the fact that many of its foundational assumptions are beliefs, not based on any testable "facts". For instance, what if the base reality was that we were all living in a giant video game? Then we'd be missing something vital, which is that the ultimate controlling force in our universe isn't the laws of physics, but the creator(s) of the game we're in. The

Dungeon Master, if you will.

In more recent times, some thinkers have begun to suggest just that. Philosophers like Nick Bostrom, scientists like Neil deGrasse Tyson, Rizwan Virk, and Jaron Lanier, and visionaries like Elon Musk are among them – people who have suggested that this might all be a giant video game. The technology of virtual embodiment has launched us in the direction of creating games in which we can become convinced we are someone else. And oddly, this isn't a new idea. The ancient Hindus held a myth that, translated into gaming terms, looks something like this:

> *There is a great, unknowable Dungeon Master. This DM is not something we can imagine, explain, or put into any conceptual box. It is not a "he" or a "she", it is not defined by any rules or concepts, it is not anything we can ever know.*
>
> *This DM becomes the world, in an interactive act of creation. DM becomes trees, insects, stars, televisions, pineapples, emotions, concepts, and even you and me. DM becomes the great drama of the world, and DM allows itself to become "lost" in these becomings, much as we become lost in a role-playing adventure or a good movie. If the game or movie is immersive enough, for a few moments we can forget who we really are, and that's exactly what DM does.*

Except DM can create a game that is more elaborate and detail-rich than anything we humans have yet dreamed of.

You and I, as human beings, have the unique power to remember who we are, to "awaken" from the Matrix, to take the red pill. To realize we are in a role-playing game, and perhaps, eventually, to come to the deepest of realizations — that we **are** *the Dungeon Master (though it is essential to realize that it is not our characters who are DM, but instead another, deeper Self that is hiding within us).*

Might we all be characters in a virtual reality game, lost in the gameplay so deeply that we have forgotten we're playing? Indeed, would there be any way to prove the following letter wasn't true?

Hi. It's you, writing to you. I know this will be difficult to believe, but your name is actually Morgan. This is Morgan (me), writing to you (also me).

Confused yet?

I decided to play the latest game put out by Beyul Studios. It's called 'Satori'. The game is set in the first half of the 21st century (the year is actually 2144 right now, about a hundred years after the setting of Satori), and I'm playing, well . . . you. I know the game might not seem very fun. No dragons, no magic, and the dramas can feel rather mundane. But the game is about remembering who you are. That's it. The whole game. As your character, you feel relatively powerless, right? Life just happens to you, and it's often not that good. But as you remember who you are, you'll gain more control over the game.

I decided to slip this letter into some element of your game – a book you're going to think you're reading. I'll actually slip a lot of these clues into your game, but this will be one of the most direct ones, where I tell you exactly what's going on.

To play the game, I signed on, then took a pill that initiates the game. In my lifetime, the game lasts only about six seconds, but to you it will seem like the space of a human life. This is because the gamepill hacks into the area of my brain that governs time perception, and can make "eternity in an hour", as Blake said (he's one of my/your favorite poets).

When I took the gamepill, it initiated the game process in my mind. Within slightly more than three seconds, it altered my memories and perception of reality. I forgot who I was. I was implanted with memories (all the memories you consider to be "yours"). And the game began.

Your subjective experience is that you were born, have grown up, and still have life ahead of you. In actuality, however, your game began very recently.

Almost everything that you "remember" happening in your life before this is just implanted memory, to give you the sensation of being a "real person". From this moment forward, you are playing the game. WE are playing the game. Or equally, I am playing the game through you. I have forgotten Morgan, and become you. Now I'm lost in the game, believing myself to be you, and the only clues I have to solve this game are this book, this letter, and the clues interspersed throughout the rest of the game.

We are in second four of six. The entire gameplay will take place in this second, and then, when you come to the end of your life, I will "wake up" to being Morgan again. This takes about two seconds for the gamepill to come to an end and me to return to normal perceptions.

Now you might be thinking something akin to this – Morgan, why did you choose THIS game? I mean, bills to pay, pollution, wars, and lots of boredom. Wasn't there a game about battling space aliens or becoming a super-mage?

Well, I sort of got bored of those. And Satori is special. It's a multiverse game, where if you succeed in solving this level, there are successive levels that open up. Successive games, really. It's the ultimate role playing game, unlike anything before it. Solve Satori, and we gain entrance to a whole multiverse, where we will essentially be like Cowan Faol (who you will meet soon in this book), able to sculpt worlds and play within them.

So . . . it all falls on you. Who, paradoxically, is me. We're smart, and I think you're probably getting this, at least a little. The rest of this book will make things more clear.

Let's do this!

You'll have four voices speaking with you in this book. The first is me, Kenton, your main narrator. Another you've already met. That's Morgan, who is a far cry from solving the game, but brings important perspective since Morgan knows the basics of what's going on. The next is Cowan Faol, a character of mine from another world, who fully "awakened" to the game he was playing. He'll be able to give you some serious wisdom and guidance. And finally, DM. DM is the voice of the great "something" behind all of this, the big game-maker, the one that is, just like Morgan, losing itself in the characters of you and me, and calling us back to knowing who we really are.

Morgan Speaks – *Gameplay begins NOW, my friend. Almost everything in your "past" is just implanted memory. You can let it all go, and start fresh in this moment. You are NOT limited by your past, so don't use it as an excuse. For anything. Adventure forward!*

chapter one
WE ARE ALL GAMERS

As Rebecca and I explored Eastern thought, pondered on the movie *The Matrix*, and continued finding ways to make our own role-playing more immersive, we had a startling realization one day. The realization was that *we are all role-playing*.

It's kind of ironic, actually. The very people who might criticize your gaming or role-playing are themselves role-playing. They just don't know it. Think about it for a moment. What is a role-playing game? A bunch of people get together, and their actions revolve around a set of rules and behaviors that are dictated by whatever game they are playing. The social interaction doesn't "work" unless everyone agrees to this basic idea that we play by the rules. In an RPG (role playing game), this means we all listen to the Dungeon Master (or equivalent), honor the dice rolls, and play the parts of our characters. In video games, we won't be successful unless we follow the basic map, fight the right people or monsters, and solve the puzzles or collect the artifacts that the game is built around.

Both of these systems, the RPG and the video game, create scenarios that encourage compulsory behavior. In the RPG, that compulsion is largely social, because our friends will get more than a little upset if we're supposed to be playing Hector the Barbarian and we start acting like Jar Jar Binks. In the video game, we simply won't be able to advance if we don't pick up health packs, kill the aliens, or perform other "trigger" actions that allow the game to go on.

But what about Bob the Plumber, who lives down the road and always teases you because you play too many video games? Well, he's playing a role-playing game too. It's a bigger one, played by a lot of players. There are actual rulebooks, in the forms of laws and statutes. And there is social pressure to behave according to the game's norms – if Bob decides he wants to dress up like Hector the Barbarian and roam the streets, he's probably going to end up in jail or on the couch of a psychiatrist.

Furthermore, different "cultures" are playing different kinds of games. In some of these games, you wouldn't be welcome at all. In others, you'd have to learn different languages, customs, and behaviors if you wanted to fit in. Stand on a corner in Madison, Wisconsin and start preaching about worshiping the Flying Spaghetti Monster, and you'll probably just get a mixture of laughter, glares, and curious onlookers. Do the same thing in North Korea, and your head may very well be inconveniently separated from your body.

Of course, this big RPG we're all playing seems more real than *Assassin's Creed*. Because we all believe strongly that we ARE our characters, it's a very big deal if we get thrown in prison, are diagnosed with cancer, or can't pay our bills. In fact, this RPG is so masterfully crafted and immersive that 99% of people call it the "real world" and don't realize they are in an RPG. The other 1% is composed mostly of mystics, Ninja Jedi Zen masters, Satorians, and world travelers who have seen enough of other cultures to realize that human rules and customs, clothing and expected behaviors, are surprisingly diverse and sometimes arbitrary (though there are similarities in most cultures to be sure).

Bob the Plumber is playing his role. He really thinks he is Bob, and he really thinks he's a plumber. He mostly obeys the rules and expectations of his role as plumber and husband, though sometimes he sneaks food from the refrigerators of kitchens he is fixing, and sometimes he sneaks onto his computer to watch some porn when his wife isn't home. He believes money is real, even though money clearly has no value unless the people around him *believe* it has value (he can prove this to himself by taking a foreign currency and trying to buy something at Walmart), and he spends a lot of time worrying about finances. Mostly, he thinks life is pretty boring, and wishes it could be more exciting. Thus the fridge thefts and porn. He has some dreams about doing something wild and crazy and adventurous, but the rules and expectations of the game pin him down, holding him hostage. And he will never break free, because he takes the game very, very seriously, and believes it to be truly real.

How many of us are like Bob the Plumber, feeling trapped in lives we don't really enjoy, thinking that there must be more to life than earning just enough money to pay this month's bills, then repeating, month after month after month?

It goes deeper. The real beauty of this RPG we're all playing is that it uses the Russian nesting doll technique of layering games within games. We are lost in our roles as plumbers, hackers, car mechanics, or IT experts, but then we get trapped one level deeper when we watch *The Avengers* and lose ourselves in the movie, or get drunk and lose ourselves in the alcohol, or play *Halo* and lose ourselves in blasting the Covenant. Novels, TV series, and paper-and-dice RPGs do the same thing, sweeping us away from the main RPG we're playing into a game-within-a-game.

But note that RPGs and video games are qualitatively different than alcohol or movies. How? They are *interactive*. They are *participatory*. They've been put here as a direct example for us, to show us almost exactly how the bigger RPG, the one other people call the "real world" and Morgan calls Satori, works. In a movie, you just watch. You may feel a lot of emotions, getting excited, sad, and upset. But you are irrelevant to the movie, and your desires and actions have no effect on the outcomes. In a video game, however, you become your character. You can grow in power, or diminish in power. You explore your world, you talk to people, you collect things, you uncover clues, and you move forward in a story that wouldn't be told if you weren't playing. You are a vital part of the video game. In fact, with single-player games, the game wouldn't even be running if you weren't there. In ways we will come to understand more fully in this book, you and the game are so inextricably bound together that while you are playing, we might even call you and the game "one".

If you begin talking with other people about the possibility that this world is "illusion", that it's all a big role-playing game, the mass of people will probably think you're crazy. But other gamers will be more likely to see behind the matrix. Because they already have the context of gaming in their psyche, they'll be able to see that things like money, celebrity status, stocks and bonds, property ownership, political positions, the value of artifacts like gold or jewels – these only have "reality" if enough people believe in them and are playing by the rules. But all it takes is a governmental collapse, some social shifts, or just enough people changing their minds, and "real" things are suddenly seen as they are. For example, in early 1900's Germany when inflation made the German mark so worthless that people used bundles of marks as fuel for their stoves.

Why does this matter? Why is it important that we gamers have this special insight? Well, it's illustrated nicely in *The Matrix* when we see the mass of people rushing along the streets to work, completely lost in the illusion. They have no idea what is really going on, and are essentially slaves to the system they are working in. It doesn't matter if they are homeless, a top CEO, the most beloved of celebrities, or the president – they are all equally lost in the game, completely at the whim of the system they are caught in.

When we realize the nature of the game, the game FEELS different to us. When the person walking next to you sees a celebrity, they will experience an unconscious mental and physiological reaction, breaking into a sweat, getting excited, and being willing to do almost anything the celebrity wants. You, on the other hand, will see the celebrity as just another person who, by the whims of the system, is in a temporary and illusory state of popularity.

Other conventions of the game, such as money (a big one that causes a LOT of issues for most of us) will also lose much of their power over you. And even more significantly, this initial realization opens the door to new ways to interact with the game – things that can seem almost magical. Essentially, it's like learning how to code, and beginning to be able to mod your game.

DM Speaks -- *We are playing a game together, you and I. I have become you, and as you successively recognize your true nature, the rules of the game will change from something that binds you into something that liberates you.*

---

chapter two

THE STORY OF COWAN FAOL

Cowan was my first character in the world of Carador that Rebecca and I created. And I'm still playing him today, thirty years later. He started his life as a teenager fascinated by magic. His family were peasants, and the political climate was such that magic was strictly illegal, with magical practices only allowed to royally sanctioned individuals. Nevertheless, he found a teacher who taught him some minor spells, and his magical career began. With a nearly photographic memory and a high aptitude for magic, the basics of magic came easily to him. His creativity furthered his skills, helping him realize that a simple spell, such as a color-changing spell, could have wide applications, from making something "disappear" in its environment (changing something to the same color as its background) to frightening away potential enemies (by suddenly changing his eyes red). He became an adventurer, finding old grimoires and learning more spells, with a leaning toward illusions. He also studied worldly skills, from sailing to cooking, and eventually built himself a small catamaran-style ship he called *Tempest*. He sailed *Tempest* back and forth to the land of Moraithe, a tropical paradise that he loved to visit, and during his long solo sails, he studied magic for ten to fifteen hours each day.

He eventually met a woman named Lillian, who had ambitions to change the political climate from its repressive, male-dominated state to a more enlightened state where common people could have a chance to improve their lot, and importantly for Cowan, magic would no longer be illegal. Cowan joined her in overthrowing the regime, and Lillian became Queen Lillian, loved by the people and feared by other governments around the world that still held to the old, repressive ways.

Hailed as one of the world's most powerful mages, Cowan was now a shapeshifter, and could take the form of anything from a flea to a mountain dragon. He had learned to "mod" and create his own spells, and with the use of a "force illusion" spell he invented, he essentially made his illusions real. Until he met Lydavia, however, he didn't know how limited his magic still was.

Lydavia was famed as a horse breeder and vintner,

and almost no one knew she was a magic shaper – someone so adept at magic that they no longer used spells, reagents, or rituals. She simply shifted reality to her will. Through her coaching, Cowan began a journey into "unlearning" all the magic he had learned. Eventually he surpassed even Lydavia, though this was not for any ambition of power. Rather, it was a natural unfolding of his spiritual journey, as he began to see his connection with all things, the illusory nature of reality, and even the illusion of "Cowan". When his will was relinquished, he discovered a way of being with the world that no longer involved his "self" wanting to change things. This part might be difficult to understand due to the constraints of our language, but if he wanted a bowl of ice cream, he didn't "want" it into existence, as he would have in the past with a spell. Instead, he found himself pleasantly surprised to find a bowl of ice cream on the table.

Cowan's "power" grew so profound that eventually he gave up trying to help and rescue people around the world (to most people he was a hero, though to much of the still-repressive establishment he was the devil incarnate). Instead, he created or evolved a new world within the world, where magic was commonplace, humans and fae could live together in harmony, and most of the evils of the world became distant memories. He became a world-creator.

And the important part for us to know is that Cowan

Faol's journey is our journey, should we choose to follow it.

Cowan Faol Speaks – *Here's a secret. We are ALL magic shapers. Everyone around you is creating a reality. They just don't know it, and thus the realities they create can sometimes look pretty bleak. First, wake yourself up until you realize you're a magic shaper. Then awaken others who also desire to know what they are!*

---

chapter three

ULTIMATE POWER MEANS NO POWER (AND VICE VERSA)

There is one vital thing Cowan discovered – conscious magic shaping can't happen if you are locked into ego and will. Believing you are a singular person, separate from all others, injects your mind with severe limitations. This Little Me is so concerned with preserving and bettering itself that it creates a constant lack (so it can keep trying to preserve and better itself). Lack and powerlessness is built into the belief system. It is only when we release all our desires and thoughts of self-need that power like Cowan's comes to be. If Cowan collapsed into fear, blame, and self-servingness, his powers would diminish. But since Cowan has come to fully understand that he is you and me and all the people and things and events in Carador, his power is almost unlimited.

Herein lies the greatest secret that shapes this big

RPG we're all in. *It is desire for bettering our own lot that keeps us locked into a drama of never having the things we really want.* This is the master key to solving Satori. We must release our ego and will, and we do this by remembering what's really happening here, and who we really are. And paradoxically, in doing so we come to "be" ourselves again. Cowan didn't disappear. He still is Cowan, still world-renowned as a great mage, still adventuring, and still enjoying ice cream. Similarly, when we realize who we are, we will still be ourselves. The only difference is that instead of this RPG seeming real and serious and terrible, it will become a game where we can fearlessly play and have fun.

Wait a moment. Is this just intention-manifestation wrapped in a different package?

Not at all. In the journey set before us in this book, we may come to find that we can wield a sort of life-altering magic, even in this world of cars and taxes and leaky faucets. But this emerges only by following a completely different route than the one laid out through most interpretations of intention-manifestation. Intention-manifestation stresses fulfillment through amassing externals, actually locking us deeper into Satori's distractions. However, as we release our clinging to our Little Me, our desire to manifest millions of dollars and shiny new yachts evaporates. Instead, we find that fulfillment circumvents the need for all the things that others cling to. While others are trapped in the superficial quest set forth by Satori (better your lot by making money, saving for retirement, and buying that yacht), you will see that this superficial quest is just a veil hiding the deeper, real quest that Satori is all about.

Morgan Speaks – *The "enemy" in Satori is distraction. The game will keep you distracted chasing money, chasing approval, chasing Facebook likes and people and sparkly new things. If you look around you, you'll see that everyone is basically spending all their time chasing things. You can do this during your whole Satori gaming experience, until you "die" in the game, and then we lose. But in Satori, when you stop chasing those things, you'll get more of them anyway. The trick is that we have to genuinely stop the chase. If we stop chasing things while secretly hoping that there will be a "payoff", nothing will change. That's why Satori is such a challenging game.*

---

chapter four
WHY THE JEDI ROCK

Rebecca and I explored all sorts of religious traditions and wisdom ways in our spiritual journey, from Christianity to Vedanta to Taoism to Zen. But of all of these, which do you think is most useful when we are playing Satori? Well, Jediism of course!

The Jedi (I'm talking about the heart of their Way, not how it manifested in actual practice in the canon) held to a tradition that has many similarities to other wisdom ways, with an emphasis on being loving, peaceful, and compassionate, but doing so while listening to the reasons of a higher power. First, it's nice that their higher power is the Force, which does away with all the awkward parts of trying to picture the Ultimate as a big grey-haired dude in the sky who has a surprising level of foibles and insecurities for a god. Taoism comes close to Jediism in this way – the Tao and the Force are both indescribable in words, unbound by human limitations or ideas, and yet serve to guide our lives in powerful ways, especially when we learn to listen and sense that guidance.

In essence, we might call this emphasis on being good to others "service". This is the idea of helping our fellow human beings (and plants and animals and ecosystems) however we can. This sense of love and compassion and service are vital – not only because they open the doors to more "power" (as we discussed in Cowan's story), but because it FEELS good to help others. Studies show pretty clearly that if we do something self-serving, it creates momentary, fleeting happiness. Do something for others, and we receive long-lasting happiness in exchange.

As I said, lots of traditions emphasize service. But few focus on strengthening yourself so that you can better be of service. Think about it. Christianity emphasizes serving others, and most churches host mission trips where people go to sometimes sketchy places, such as disaster areas, to help people rebuild their lives. But Christianity puts no emphasis on push-ups (which would allow someone to lift more and thus be better able to rebuild homes), no emphasis on martial arts (which would allow someone to feel more secure in sketchy areas of the world and thus be able to operate more confidently), no emphasis on meditation (which would allow someone to be more energized, compassionate, and clear-headed in stressful conditions).

The Jedi (and to some extent the Shaolin monks and some types of yogis) can't get away with avoiding their push-ups. It is understood that they will better be able to step in and help others, to confront dangerous situations, to operate under stress, and to make clear judgments if they are spiritually, mentally, and physically strong. The more they can cultivate inner and outer strength and resilience, the more they can be of service to others. Thus their spirituality is intimately tied in with physical conditioning, lightsaber training, meditation, and other rigors.

If we use the Jedi as guideposts, we'll gain even more benefits in Satori. A strong body will allow adventures; with swift reactions, good muscle tone, and some cardio, we open up the door to parkour, sparring, rock climbing, mountain biking, tree climbing, and more. We're simply able to experience more fun in the world. A strong mind helps us to develop heightened awareness, which allows us to see through the matrix into what's really going on. And emotional resilience means we won't be pushed around by every influence and distraction that comes into our game. In short, we'll be able to "play" more parts of the game, and we'll be better able to solve Satori's riddles and move forward in our journey.

Cowan Faol Speaks – *To become a world-crafter, I had to give up being a mage. I had to give up magic, and my clinging to my Little Me. You've probably placed yourself into many boxes in the past. Perhaps "Christian", or "gamer", or "loser", or "good person". These labels hold power, so use them wisely. And understand that in the end, all of our labels must be seen for what they are – just masks we put on, that have little to do with who is behind the disguise.*

chapter five

THE JOURNEY BEGINS

I'm going to re-emphasize, right here, that love and compassion are essential if we want to advance in Satori. This can be tough for gamers. We're often used to being criticized, and many of us feel like we never quite "fit in" with the rest of society. We may have found a sense of community with other gamers, but often those relationships aren't flesh-and-blood, and rather are developed in the context of our games which often means online. At ReWild University, in our 11-month and 4-month wilderness immersion programs, many of our Forest Monks came to us extremely addicted to video games. They would easily label themselves "addicts", and accept that designation from others.

For many of us, it can feel like "us against them", or even "me against them". "Them" can be our parents, our peers, our teachers, our friends – all the people around us who don't game in the conventional sense (although, as we already discussed, they're all gaming without knowing it).

This division serves to enhance our Little Me, that part of us that feels like we are miniature drivers in our squishy bodies. That part of us that, in believing it's "me against the world", develops a belief system that keeps finding problem after problem, keeps experiencing being judged, keeps itself wrapped in a secure little blanket of blaming others and feeling victimized.

Thus the first step on our journey is perhaps the most painful and most powerful. You see, we desperately want to be told that we're special, that we're important. (And in a way, as a gamer, you are.) But before we can see how we are special, we have to first see that we are no different from anyone else. This is the first step in transforming the Little Me – to stop comparing ourselves, both positively and negatively, to others.

By doing this, we begin building bridges where before we were tearing them down. We start the process of no longer clinging to our Little Mes, and see the first glimpses of oneness with all the other elements in the Satori RPG.

This is tough because we have probably learned to identify with our feelings of victimhood, superiority, or "otherness". If we give up those identities, what is left?

Who are we?

As we'll discover, when we gain the courage to give up those flimsy, cobbled-together labels we've been placing over ourselves, we part the veil and begin the process of discovering that we are much, much more than those labels could ever dream of being.

How do we build those bridges? Well, first we get to meet one of our most powerful "weapons" in Satori. This is our ability to place our mental focus where we want it. Learning to do this is like learning to put the lightsaber blade where we want it. Without this basic skill, we're going to be at the whim of Satori's distractions, as Morgan warned. With it, we gain the Jedi's lightsaber, the warrior's sword, the mage's grimoire.

Wait! Are you saying that you have ADHD? Or that your mind is basically like a dancing monkey, focusing everywhere but where you'd like it to? Join the club. Since the time of the Buddha, wisdom-speakers have been telling us that our thought-crazy mind is our worst enemy. It takes us on an endless roller-coaster of anxieties, dramas, what-ifs, fears, and insecurities.

Well, my Satorian, those days are about to come to an end. IF you are up to putting in some hard work. And I mean hard. If solving Satori were easy, we'd all be Ninja Jedi Zen Masters.

Morgan Speaks – *When you take the gamepill and enter Satori, you forget yourself and "become" your character. You have your (my) mind, but it's buried under your character's mind, which is pre-programmed with a bunch of liabilities. One of the biggest is lack of focus, because that lack of focus makes you vulnerable to just about every distraction Satori can throw at you. Sharpen your focus, and every single challenge Satori uses to keep you lost in the game becomes weaker.*

---

chapter six

DEVELOPING MENTAL FOCUS

Games almost always feature objects that are vitally important if the characters are to get anywhere. Guns, wands, swords, maps, med packs . . . we might loosely call all of these things "tools". Focus is a mental tool, and trying to play Satori without it is like trying to play *Halo* without a gun, or being a warrior without any weapons. Possible, perhaps, but without these basic tools, things are MUCH more difficult.

If you're like many of us, you may think that there is no way you'll ever have good mental focus. After all, the sad fact is that we're all crazy. That's right. Loony. Bonkers. Bananas.

As I wrote this, my family was on a seven-month-long adventure in Hawai'i. On the Big Island, there is a town called Pahoa. And in that town are many people struggling with mental illness. When Rebecca was in Australia in her teens, these people were called "spinners". Drive in to Pahoa, and you'll see a small but significant percentage of the residents talking to themselves, having kung fu battles with imaginary people, or walking about in a drug-induced haze. It's easy to think that Pahoa has more spinners than other places. But the truth is that we're ALL spinners. That is, if being crazy is being "in your own world" and oblivious to the "real world" all around us.

It seems obvious that someone is crazy when they are screaming and pointing to a pink elephant that you can't see. But if you think about it, it's just as crazy (just not as dramatic) when a businessman is walking down the sidewalk imagining the meeting that's going to happen tomorrow. In his head, he's in another reality, fabricating scenarios and arguments, most of which will probably never happen at the actual meeting. Usually, he's not in command of these fantasies. They just "happen", and he might stumble into someone, make a wrong turn, or almost get hit by a car because he's so lost in his imaginary reality. He may not be talking out loud like some of the people in Pahoa, but instead he's talking loudly in his head, busy in an imaginary reality that he believes to be real. In essence, it's really no different than the pink elephant.

So we have the mass of people (except for a few Ninja

Jedi Zen Masters, yogis, and advanced Satorians) walking around talking to themselves, either out loud or silently in their heads. Being a spinner is normal.

Does this mean that any thinking or imagining we do is bad? Not at all. In fact, imagination is one of our most powerful human abilities. The difference is focus. Are we able to put our minds where we want them, and to use imagination consciously? Or does our imagination rule over us, commanding our thoughts and driving us into anxiety and mindlessness?

As I mentioned, the Buddha was talking about this almost 3,000 years ago, and the Hindus before that. Buddha noted that we're all in a constant dialog with ourselves in our heads, and that engaging in that dialog trains our minds into a state of distraction. We practice the art of mind-chatter for ten to twelve hours every day, and we get really, really good at it. We are ninjas of distraction.

A mind that is chattering is no longer aware of what's going on around it. And as we'll see, it's important to be tuned in to Satori if we want to see all the clues unfolding around us. Would we try to take on the toughest level of our favorite video game while also putting together a puzzle? Of course not. We're super-focused on the gameplay.

It's no different with Satori. Focus on the gameplay, and we not only enjoy the game further, but we advance more quickly. Live in a state of distraction, and all we notice are the stories in our heads.

Developing focus, as I said, is tough. Really tough. But the good news is that some simple exercises will begin sharpening your sword of focus. And you don't need to become Jedi-level tomorrow. Every tiny bit of focus you develop will help you on your way. You can begin with the Dancing Monkey Meditation.

Dancing Monkey Meditation

You can do this anytime. When you wake up, when you're waiting in line . . . and if you want to get some bonus points, use it to interrupt some distraction, like a TV commercial or a negative story you're telling in your head.

Look around you, and select one thing. A tiny point is best. A scuff on a wall, a knot in some wood, the button on a game controller. Stare at it, and keep your mind on it for the space of a slow inhale (about 4 or 5 seconds). As you exhale, let your eyes drift to some new spot around you. Then, for the inhale, keep your mind focused on that new thing. Repeat, and just keep going. You can do it for a minute or for ten minutes, whatever you like. More important than the duration of each session is getting in the habit of doing it regularly, even if it's just for three or four breaths.

You'll probably find that you can focus using this method MUCH more powerfully than you could when you just try to stay focused on one thing. Why? Because we're catering to the dancing monkey in our heads. It likes to switch from one thing to another in rapid succession. So we let it switch, but we sneak in focus training at the same time by holding it on one spot for a few seconds. Your mind probably won't resist much, because you're letting it get away with its old habits while secretly training it. Kind of like putting someone who doesn't like to exercise on a trampoline. In the right context, they'll be laughing and having a great time, hardly noticing that they are getting a great cardio and leg workout.

Cowan Faol Speaks – *I remember learning my first spell, a simple color-change spell. My teacher could summon cinnamon rolls from thin air, and I was limited to changing small areas to different hues. I can recall a moment when I stood at a mental crossroads. I could feel a sense of futility building inside of me, because it had taken so much work just to master this simple spell. Would I ever be anywhere close to the power of my teacher? As you develop focus, it will probably feel much the same, like you're making baby steps and not really getting anywhere. But focus is THE power that will make all the difference in Satori, and move you from being literally pushed around by the world to developing an uncanny ability to shape the world around you. Practice diligently, and know that it will pay off in unexpected ways.*

---

chapter seven
BUILDING BRIDGES

Remember how it was going to be very important to start building bridges instead of tearing them down, since our connection with other people (and everything else) is one of the keys to solving Satori? And how we need mental focus to initiate the building? Well, here's why. Because as you learn how to focus your mind, you get to take control of what influences your mind.

In other words, if we look around at people and think about how lame they are and how much they hate us, that becomes the "reality" we hold in our minds, and because we'll treat people accordingly, they will tend to react accordingly, reinforcing the idea in our heads. But if we look around at people and see similarities, we'll find that we begin to treat them differently, and they begin to treat us differently in turn. It's the basic principle of going through a check-out line, smiling at the cashier, and asking them how their day is going. Do that, and you'll have a higher percent chance of them smiling back and appearing to be in a good mood. Walk through with a scowl on your face and barely acknowledge them, and you'll have a very different memory of what that person is like.

In a way, we have a lot of power over how the people around us appear.

So how do we build bridges? We use that new power of focus to direct our mind to similarities rather than differences.

We already have a great one. We're all spinners! This puts a humorous spin on everything. You and I are fellow residents in a great big loony bin. Everyone around us, from the president of the United States to that checkout guy at the corner store to our friends and family and ourselves – we're all crazies. Excellent! We have something that is similar for all of us.

We're also all gamers, as we've already talked about. Some of us know it, and others don't, but we're all gamers. You're living in a world where everyone is a fellow gamer.

Put your mind to it. What other similarities can you find? Make a list. And then, start using your newfound mental focus (even if your powers seem meager right now) to direct your mind toward those similarities. Make it into a game. Have FUN with it.

This is important, because our minds have well-worn pathways of habit, and if you're like most of us, your habit is to look negatively at people around you, comparing yourself to them, criticizing them, and being jealous of them. We must retrain our minds. Every time it goes on "default" and tries to focus on the differences, switch gears. Focus on a similarity from your list.

Don't be too hard on yourself. When you first start training your mind, you might have quite a few failures. That's okay. We've spent years and years developing these habits of seeing separation. It's going to take some time to learn to see differently. But as we do, we plant seeds, and each one has the potential to grow into a powerful tree. Indeed, into a forest.

DM Speaks – *Everything you take into your mind becomes part of its composition. Others will gladly dictate your mind's content for you if you let them. But you have the choice to take the helm, if you develop the power of focus. Choose to place your focus on things that bring you closer to your true nature.*

---

chapter eight
WHAT VIDEO GAMES AND RPGs REALLY ARE

Long, long ago, when humans' most advanced technology was fire, stories were told around the flames. It's a part of human nature to weave tales. Over time, those stories developed into novels and the first motion pictures. But we might term all of these types of storytelling as "non-participatory". What I mean by that is that as the listener (as opposed to the storyteller), your role is simply to listen or watch the story unfold.

Developing in parallel were traditions of historical re-enactment that incorporated improvisation (we know that such things were practiced in China over 2,000 years ago) and commedia dell'arte, which were "participatory" in the sense that instead of an active storyteller and passive listeners, each participant on the stage played a role and could influence the course or outcome of the story, often with input from the audience. This blurred the line between storyteller and listener.

It wasn't until the 1960's and 70's when the concept of RPGs emerged in the modern sense, culminating in the commercial release of TSR's Dungeons and Dragons in 1974. Since then, video games have emerged and become increasingly immersive. Today, of course, we have an endless variety of worlds to explore and characters to become.

The important point for us is that video games and RPGs are qualitatively different from games like chess or cards, and also different from other "entertainments" like movies or novels. Notice that a novel or movie is non-participatory. You watch, and can only hope that things turn out the way you want them. But nothing you do will change the outcome. In a video game or RPG, things are much more participatory (to a greater or lesser extent depending on the type of game). You take on a role, and the story can't move forward without you. In open-world games especially, our characters can have an enormous influence on not only our own experiences, but others' experiences as well (and even, in some cases, the world as a whole). This distinction, though it isn't black-and-white (you may notice that chess is much more participatory than watching *The Avengers*, but much less than playing *Assassin's Creed Odyssey*), will help us to become more participatory in our gameplay.

It's very likely that our ancient ancestors lived in a very participatory universe, in that they saw themselves as intricately entwined with other animals and plants, with the elements of nature, and with each other. This created a participatory mindset in them, which meant the world looked very different to them than it does to us. It *felt* different. By the end of this book, you'll have discovered much more about this participatory mindset, so I won't try to describe it here. But in short, when you live in a participatory mindset (and thus a participatory world), you don't feel as lonely, isolated, victimized, anxious, or fearful.

To understand why, it's easier to look at our current non-participatory mindset (and thus non-participatory world) that we're much more familiar with. We've all watched movies, right? They are entertaining, fun, and in modern times, the special effects are getting so awesome that they're starting to look fake again.

Criticism of modern Hollywood productions aside, it's clear to see that movies are relatively non-participatory. When we watch one, we are observers. We may have physiological reactions, we may laugh or cry or cheer, but the participation only goes in one direction. As we just noted, nothing we do will change the ending of the movie, and if we leave the theater, the movie will go on without us. We might enjoy movies, but somewhere, deep down, we know that in the system that is a movie, we don't matter except to donate money to the movie producers. We're just there to passively observe.

Movies are a symptom of an overall non-participatory mindset in our culture. Most interpretations of modern science (unless you read the works of some of the more visionary physicists or computer scientists), which have strongly shaped our mindsets, have instilled the dogma of a non-participatory mindset. We are the product of random movements, we come into the world for a brief flash, and then we die. In the big scheme of things, we're irrelevant. Humans themselves don't really matter. The Earth doesn't matter. In the end, after all, the universe is just going to collapse back upon itself and nothing we've ever done or accomplished will have any meaning.

In the non-participatory world, you are largely powerless and utterly insignificant. Is it any wonder that so many people feel lost in a sense of hopelessness and anxiety? Any wonder that as our world gets more addicted to non-participatory entertainment, we see increases in mental illness and depression?

Now, if you love movies, don't despair. You don't have to give them up. We just have to learn to make them more participatory (more on that later). But know that in general, when we watch a movie or read a novel, we reinforce the non-participatory mindset in ourselves. When we play a video game or RPG or LARP (live action role playing game), we reinforce a participatory mindset in ourselves. And as we move forward in our journey, it's essential that we begin to tip the scales in favor of participatory. In fact, the more we can start to see the world in a participatory way, the more we'll start to see the world change around us, and the clues to solving Satori will begin to appear more clearly.

We're starting to see that to solve Satori, we must realize that games are not ends in themselves, not just here to pass time or distract us from life. Instead, they are powerful tools and clues to the nature of Satori itself. Of course, if used unconsciously they have the power to be little different from movies, just serving to drag us deeper into Satori's illusions. But if we use them with wisdom and intention, they cease to become distractions, and instead become doorways into Satori's deepest secrets.

We can unleash their power. To do so, we use them to inspire us to role-play and adventure in the main Satori game, not just in the games-within-games that Satori delivers.

Morgan Speaks – *Satori has games-within-games, all meant to distract you from solving Satori. Yet some of those games, especially participatory ones, are actually vital clues. They mirror exactly what's going on in Satori itself. Let those games stir up your spirit of adventure, and then use them as inspiration to explore Satori. After all, Satori is the largest, most immersive open world game ever created. It is totally convincing. You didn't even know you were playing until I told you, right? Well, maybe you had an inkling. But now that you really know, it's time to see the games for what they are – training grounds for learning to adventure in Satori just like you adventure within the games-within-the-game.*

chapter nine

SOME TERMINOLOGY

It's probably time for a station break. You see, I'm writing this in the English language, and English is profoundly lacking in words to describe the more subtle states of mind and concepts we'll be encountering on our journey. So let's begin a little glossary, and as we continue forward into future chapters, I'll include more.

Satori – *The "game" we are all playing, whether we know it or not. The only goal in the game is to "wake up" to what's actually happening and become conscious role-players, and from there to remember who we really are. Also references the "world" in the game.*

Satorian – *You and I, those who know we're in Satori and are on a journey to solve its riddles.*

Forest Monk – *Students who came to ReWild University and trained in many of the same skills as Satorians, only with a nature-oriented focus.*

Games-Within-the-Game – *Role-playing games within the main RPG of Satori. This includes pen-and-paper RPGs, LARPing, and RPG-based video games.*

Distractions – *The main "enemies" in Satori, coming in various guises. Many of these are obvious, like TV, texting, porn, drugs, or drama. But others are more subtle, like money, desire for attention, and basic drives like hunger or thirst. Note that all distractions can become clues, but it takes intensive training and consciousness in order to transform them, especially the more addictive and subtle ones.*

Clues – *Elements of Satori that reveal, in gross or subtle ways (usually very, very subtle), the pathway toward solving Satori.*

Tools – *Various techniques, conscious beliefs, and deliberate habits that serve to guide us toward solving Satori.*

Participatory Mindset — *A mindset that recognizes its interconnection with all other elements of the universe, and is freed from blame, victimhood, and feeling like the Little Me. In the participatory mindset, we become an active participant in everything that happens to us and around us in Satori.*

Non-participatory Mindset – *A mindset that believes it is the Little Me, an isolated bag of flesh navigating an immense and largely hostile world. Life happens TO the non-participatory mindset, while the participatory mindset is in a mutually creative dance with life.*

Little Me – *The ego or fabricated sense of me that is formed by the non-participatory mindset. This Little Me, who most of us identify as ourselves, is fearful, anxious, lonely, and tries to fill the void through a never-ending diet of distractions. It constantly compares itself to others and judges. The Little Me believes itself to be in control of itself, but it is actually an utter slave to the directives of the game-maker. All of these directives cause the Little Me to look in the exact opposite places of where clues are to be found. It is only by overcoming the urges of the Little Me that we can cease to be slaves.*

Matrix or Veil – *The shroud of distractions that keeps people lost in the game of Satori. As we become aware of this shroud, we gather clues that allow us to see through it.*

Illusion or Delusion – *The apparent "reality" of Satori, as created by the vision of the Little Me. As we shift from the Little Me to seeing our DM nature, we see through the matrix, and begin to perceive a more truthful reality that aims us in the direction of solving Satori.*

Myth – *A story about reality as a whole or some aspect of reality that we are meant to simultaneously believe and not believe. A good myth is something we can live our lives by, while understanding that it is only pointing toward something beyond its story. A myth can be judged by how well it points us toward greater wisdom and awareness. The tricky part about myths is that if they are well constructed, they are also easy to get lost in. Lost, we become blind believers, and the myth serves only as another distraction that entraps us in the Little Me.*

Focus – *Our ability to point our minds in the directions we want, or to "look" at the elements of the world we choose. Most of us are stuck in the Little Me default autofocus. That means that we don't decide what we think, what our mind dwells upon, how to act, or much of anything. Without focus, we are slaves to others (though we believe ourselves to be our own masters). When we regain focus, we regain our ability to guide our own journey.*

DM – *This cannot be known by our Little Me mind. We can clumsily think of DM as the Dungeon Master, or creator of the Satori game. We can also think of it as our True Self. Alternately, we can think of DM as the Ultimate Reality, God, or Truth. For our purposes, we can best consider DM to be the creator of Satori, while secretly also being ourselves (but NOT our Little Me, which is simply a creation of DM used to make it challenging for us to find ourselves).*

Cowan Faol Speaks – *Language has always been a topic of interest for mages. Through language, we create our own mental reality and we affect those around us. In this way, language is a magical, creationary force. Yet few realize that it has another side, a side of deep limitation, for words "crystallize" things into concepts. Seen in their wordless state, each "thing" around us exists in its true state of full interconnection. Attach a name (word), and it is separated out into an independent "thing". This is just what we do with ourselves, to separate ourselves from the world. When I am "Cowan", I am limited. When my name and all it evokes in our consciousness is removed, I am limitless. Use words with wisdom, my friend. They can be powerful tools, but they can also be potent distractions.*

chapter ten
PLAYING SATORI

In modern times, the word "myth" has come to be synonymous with "falsehood". But a myth is actually something much deeper – a story that is simultaneously true and untrue (we'll have to get used to paradoxes as Satorians). The main function of a myth is to point us toward recognizing something that words are unable to capture.

Satori is such a myth. Are we actually lost in a giant RPG? Are we really Morgan?

Well, yes and no. So it's very important to start to loosen up our mind's insistence on black-and-white, either-or. We need to understand that yes, we are in a giant RPG, with the only meaningful objective in the game being to solve Satori's riddles and recognize who we are. And we need to understand that no, the game of

Satori is actually just a "pointer", like a finger pointing to the moon. If we believe it to be too real, we'll stare at the finger and miss entirely what the finger is pointing toward.

Pointer – *A myth, example, or description of the objective of Satori, which people often mistake for the objective itself. This is how dogma is created, by people worshipping "idols", or representations of the objective. The cross or Bible is worshipped instead of God, the Buddha worshipped instead of actually seeking enlightenment, or the myth of Satori believed in rather than actually experiencing Satori directly.*

To effectively use a myth, we need to enter this new state of believing in its reality lightly. We don't have this "believing lightly" concept in our culture, and it's missing on purpose (it's part of what makes the game of Satori so challenging). As you're getting the hang of believing lightly, the easiest path forward is to treat life like it really is a big RPG, like Morgan's letter to you is true, and that your sole purpose here is to solve Satori's riddles and discover who you really are.

But keep in the back of your mind that to truly solve Satori, you must embark into that realm of no-words, that place where we can only experience the truth, not speak of it. In this way, we find that if we approach the game of Satori only as concepts and words, we won't be led to the full truth. Satori is so ingeniously crafted that you can't solve the game by playing the game! Eventually, we must see what is beyond and behind it.

But until then, let's start learning how to play Satori to the fullest and begin to unravel some clues so that we can move closer to the participatory mindset, transform the Little Me, and start playing the ultimate game – the game that is not a game.

Okay. Satori. What's the objective? What are the rules? How do we advance?

The objective is simple, at least in words. It is to recognize, in a very true and clear way, that we are not our characters (the Little Me), and to remember who we really are. The effect, when this happens, is that we cease to be lost in the game, and the game, which for most of us wasn't really very fun in the beginning, becomes mind-blowingly amazing.

You could imagine that you start the game seeing old-style graphics on a low-res black-and-white screen. This is the gameplay almost everyone gets, even if they are popular, rich, or really really really ridiculously good looking. Getting more distractions doesn't get you a better gameplay experience or mean that you "win". That experience is only available to Ninja Jedi Zen Masters, Satorians, and the like. Once we begin to see through the veil, the game starts evolving into higher and higher resolutions, more vibrant colors, and ever-more-amazing graphics. Above and beyond that, the world of Satori begins to open to us and respond to us differently. As we enter the participatory mindset, we find that the world doesn't just "happen" to us and around us, but instead that we can explore new parts of the world and often get the world to do things for us, bring us things, or invoke wanted situations. It's almost like a sort of magic, but less like the flashy magic we envision mages using, and more like the world-shaping magic Cowan uses. As this magic unfolds in our lives, we won't be impressing anyone with stage shows like David Blaine, but instead will command a subtle but potent ability to shift our reality in ways others can't even imagine.

As for the rules, Satori is an open world. The superficial rules are the "laws of physics", and the rules put down by each culture within the game. Break those rules, and you might find yourself injured, persecuted, or even imprisoned. However, there is a deeper set of rules (or rather, anti-rules), indescribable in words but pointed to in the rest of this book, that are invoked as we advance in our gameplay.

Until we arrive at that more advanced place, remember that wherever you are, whether in your own home or in a prison cell, you're still in the game, and the main objective is just as reachable. If this understanding is taken far enough, we begin to lose our fear of getting cancer, going broke, or having any other "bad" things happen to us. Billionaire or homeless, we're in the same boat, with the same objective and essentially the same things blocking our way to that objective. In fact, for a subtle reason that we'll come to understand in the next chapter, we might actually be better off if we're homeless.

But what about advancing in Satori? That's a tricky issue, because for reasons that will become more clear as we move forward, it's not quite right to call it a "journey" or to conceptualize it as "advancing" toward something. But that's for later. Right now, we advance through making the shifts laid out before us in this book. If I did my job of writing this book well, the pathway forward will be clear.

Remember that Satori has been crafted by a supra-genius level mind, and is a highly nuanced game. This isn't for wimps. Most players will have trouble advancing past being lost in the game.

But everyone is given the same initial clues, and the same chances to see through the matrix. Since this book is in your hands, you can be assured that you've already seen many clues (even if you're not totally aware of what they were) and have already progressed in the game. These clues were put into your past memories, and you've had the awareness to piece them together enough to realize that something is going on behind-the-scenes.

This manual only comes into the game when you're ready for it. It's a major pointer. To others, the words written here might sound crazy. But to you, they are beginning a process that will become more familiar as you move forward. This process is also what I alluded to when I said that it's not really a "journey" or "advancement" that is called for. Instead, this manual has probably begun a process of *remembering*. Don't be surprised if realizations begin coming to you in flashes – things you've always known, but had somehow forgotten.

This is the process of remembering who you really are. Yes, you are your Little Me. Yes, you are Morgan, playing the game of Satori. But you are also the game maker, the crafter of Satori. You are also DM.

This is a big clue, but it also has great potential to lead you astray. So for now, file it in the back of your mind, and let's see why changing our basic approach to life is essential if we want to continue solving Satori.

DM Speaks – *In this world I have crafted for you, there are two layers. The first is the layer of the apparent, so convincing to your mind. Your mind will use any means it can to keep you believing in that first layer. But there is a second, deeper layer waiting for you once you understand that ALL the things I have created in the first layer are only pointers. Nothing more.*

---

chapter eleven

WHY PROBLEMS ARE GOOD

One thing we'll find consistently in our journey is that in order to solve Satori, we have to do things quite differently from what is considered "normal". In other words, "normal" is usually in the realm of the Little Me, the non-participatory mindset, and staying utterly lost in the lowest level of gameplay in Satori. The opposite of normal often leads us in the right direction. The trouble is that we start our gameplay pre-programmed to look in the wrong direction. So how do we break through that programming and stand a chance against Satori's many puzzles and pitfalls?

To do so, we have to flip a lot of our basic ideas about the world on their heads. This is where the focus you are developing comes into play, because it allows you to shift your gaze away from the normal things that serve as distractions in Satori. This can be uncomfortable, because those basic ideas are our security blankets, making us FEEL secure even though they are ultimately the sources of our insecurities.

One of the biggest things in this category is our effort to avoid discomfort, problems, and challenges at all costs.

Have you ever noticed that this is basically what "life is about" in the world? Everyone is doing their best to make themselves as comfortable as possible and to avoid problems.

Somewhere in the back of our minds we know this is kind of goofy. First of all it's impossible, because the game is rigged to give us problems. But secondly, even if we could reach a place of no problems, our life would then become spectacularly boring. Imagine a new video game that comes out, called *A Day In The Life*. In it, your character wakes up and eats breakfast, allowing you to choose between three different breakfast cereals in the kitchen cabinet. Then you drive to work. Then you have a long day at work during which everyone is nice to each other and everything goes great. Then you get back into the car and drive home. You get to choose from three different microwave dinners, and then eat. Then you go to bed. The next day, you repeat. Endlessly.

How long would you play the game?

Obviously, we create games with challenges, dramas, and difficult-to-reach objectives, because those challenges are fun. We all want games that are at the edge of our ability levels so that we can accomplish goals and feel good about doing something that we weren't quite sure if we were capable of doing.

So there you have the strange thing about this whole affair. In the "real world", we are putting all of our energies into making life as perfectly safe, problem-free, and comfortable as possible. This makes life terrifically dull, and thus we require "entertainment" in the form of endless movies, romance novels, and other distractions.

Are you seeing how this works? Satori is set up with our characters pre-programmed to pursue problem-free lives at almost any cost. We'll spend our whole lives in office jobs we hate just so we can have "security", and then we are lured into getting MORE lost in Satori by playing games-within-the-game or pursuing endless entertainment (aka distractions).

Of course, I also said that the game is rigged to give us problems. The creator of Satori didn't want it to be completely impossible, so the game was built with special clues in place.

Remember how I said it might be easier for the homeless person than the billionaire? Now we see why. If we are "successful" in the conventional sense, we're actually increasing our ability to engage in distractions. The billionaire can distract himself endlessly with new yachts, parties, shiny cars, second houses, and the endless stress of managing all that money and wondering if anyone would really like him if he didn't have his money (and suspecting that the answer is "probably not"). But the homeless guy has easier-to-see problems, and each of those problems is a clue in disguise.

Now, this doesn't mean you can't enjoy the fruits of gameplay in Satori. There are tons of fun things to do, experiences to have, people to meet, and foods to taste. But if those things become the objectives themselves (which they are for almost all players), then you'll never get anywhere except for lost. And when lost, all pleasures are basically the same. They give us fleeting satisfaction and implant us with desire for more, sending us on a never-ending quest to nowhere.

But if we play Satori wisely, we'll find that we are able to get more pleasure from our experiences, and thus the whole game becomes more amazing. At some point, having a pint of Ben and Jerry's or a walk in the woods will bring you MORE pleasure than the billionaire gets from buying a new yacht. And then, if you do indeed ever attain billionaire status, imagine the pleasure YOU would get from a new yacht!

So we're beginning to see life in a different light. Instead of being lost in the superficial goals of Satori, in the things that it *seems* to be about, we're seeing a bit more of the truth. And part of that truth is that problems are actually good, in that they give us opportunity for growth and advancement. Just how do they do this? Well, take the example of a really, really big problem. A diagnosis of lethal cancer. Three weeks to live.

For most players, this is the ultimate, most fearful, terrible thing that could happen. Major suck. Because they are addicted to the never-ending pursuit of comfort and security, this comes as an earth-shaking blow. All their life they've been trying to make things perfect, and then in five minutes at the doctor's office, they discover that all that work was for nothing. Note that it was the desperate seeking for security that caused the problem in the first place. If they were a Ninja Jedi Zen Master, they would have embraced insecurity (the truth of the game), and this would come as no big surprise. They could then use the next three weeks in pursuit of the ultimate objective of Satori (which they probably already have achieved if they are a Ninja Jedi Zen Master, but you get the point). However, since they are not a Ninja Jedi Zen Master, the problem isn't an opportunity, but a distraction. They'll likely spend the next three weeks in fear, denial, and anger, and then they'll die.

Game over, as Private William Hudson reminded us in *Alien*.

Cancer is a big problem that is very difficult to transform into a life lesson, but we're given all sorts of small problems that hold similar potential. How about the end-of-the-month bill we can't quite pay? Will it draw us into panic and strengthen our belief that money rules our lives? Or will we use it as an opportunity to examine our fears that are fueled by the belief in money?

This is the choice we have with every "problem" we encounter. Will it move us into fear (which draws us deeper into being lost in Satori), or will we see it as a challenge that can lead us forward?

Thus, as we move forward in Satori, we can keep in mind that if we are "successful" in the conventional sense, it is not necessarily a victory. Success is immensely more distracting than problems. Though obviously, problems can distract us as well.

Instead of trying to avoid problems at all costs, welcome them in. This will serve two functions. The first is that when one comes, you're already in the mindset to learn from it and use it as a clue. The second is that paradoxically, when you stop trying to avoid problems, Satori will start to give you lighter problems. Rebecca and I call them "gentle lessons". The trick, of course, is that if you try to welcome problems with the secret hope that you will then get fewer problems, you're just sneakily trying to avoid problems, and you'll get the same amount. But if you can truly say to Satori, "go ahead, bring it on!", and joyfully welcome in problems as gifts that help you see through the veil, then your gameplay experience in Satori will begin to transform.

Cowan Faol Speaks – *What about me? Isn't my life perfect? I've come to a place where my merest whim materializes in the world. Death, disease, and injury can't touch me, and I can have any object, food, or thing I want. Or is my life the same as that boring video game? As you progress in Satori, you'll begin to discover that problems are purposeful. My life used to be full of them, and they gave me lots of things to do. When I searched deep inside, I saw that I WANTED to have problems, because I could get lost in the drama of them. But as I began to let go of the desire for that drama, I could turn my vision from myself to others. I began to help people. But even there a trap was waiting. In desiring to help people (and be admired as the hero), I unknowingly used my magic to invoke problems in other people's lives. Again, I had to give up the reward to myself – the admiration of others. In releasing that, I came to my full power, and created a new world called Elorien where most of the forces that create problems for people were removed. I finally gained enough wisdom to stop attacking the symptoms of the problem, and instead saw what was causing the problem at its root. That cause was me, and my desire for the Little Me to feel a little bigger.*

chapter twelve

BECOMING YOUR CHARACTER

Rebecca and I used to play *Ultima IV, Quest of the Avatar*. I know. We're dating ourselves here. We loved the open world, the puzzles to solve, and finding reagents for new spells. But one of our favorite things was when we'd start a new game and create new characters. It was always exciting to answer the questions that served to generate our alternate personas. Then we'd really get into it, imagining ourselves as that person.

This is an essential part of RPGs. We "become" someone, creating a character through which we pursue goals and aspirations. Usually, our character begins with certain skills and powers, and along the way we can increase our attribute scores, gather important tools, and gain new skills.

Your character in Satori is no different, except that up

until now, you've probably not thought of yourself as a character, but rather just as "you". Thinking of yourself as a character is a serious game-changer. It gives you reasons to evolve physically, mentally, and spiritually. It frees you from many of the labels you may have put on yourself, or that others may have tried to fix upon you. And it allows you to re-invent yourself whenever you like.

For many people, the idea of thinking of themselves as a character is pretty alien. I'm me, right? But now that we know we're all role playing in a huge RPG, we realize that EVERYONE is playing a character. They're just not doing it consciously.

When our character is unconscious, it's extremely limiting. Our memories of our parental situation, friends, challenges we've had to face, etc., have all helped to craft a default character for us. Though most people could not define their character very well, a random one might sound like this:

I work in IT. I'm good at mountain biking, and fixing bikes. I'm pretty mechanical. I'm introverted, and have trouble with relationships. I have moderate anxiety, and am addicted to caffeine in any form, especially Mountain Dew. I love fantasy novels, and wish I could be an author myself. I also wish I could find a good person to share my life with, but I'm too shy to date.

This could go on, but you get the point. Most of us define ourselves (our Little Me, which equates with an unconsciously-created character) by our profession, a few personality traits, and what we like, dislike, or hope for. Many of us use culturally-created definitions to further pigeonhole ourselves, like Democrat or Libertarian, religious or atheist, gamer or non-gamer. These definitions in themselves aren't bad, but when we allow them to unconsciously define us, and then mold our thinking and actions around those labels, we become lost in our definitions, as Cowan warned us in Chapter Nine.

Things change dramatically when we realize we are role-playing and consciously craft our character. First, we realize our character isn't "real" in the sense of being "who we are" in any permanent way. This allows us to evolve character traits or even do a total character switch if we so desire. In fact, as you read the next chapters, you have the opportunity to do a full redo on your character. You are NOT required to be the same person today that you were yesterday. Yes, everyone around you will expect you to be the same (because they all believe characters are "real", and that change happens slowly if at all), but you don't have to let that limit you. Even if you've been pretty negative, mean, judgmental, or otherwise were living in ways that don't advance you in Satori, you can freely drop those old ways and start fresh, right now.

If you choose to do this, remember an important point. Your mind has been conditioned by Satori to believe the same thing everyone else is believing – that your character is WHO YOU ARE. What this means is that your mind will have habitual behaviors that might not change just because you want them to. For instance, if you lose your temper easily, and decide you want to switch that up and be ultra-patient, you might fail at it for a while because your mind is in the habit of getting angry. But once you know this secret, that you are capable of making powerful change at any time if you don't believe your character to be real, you'll find that you make changes much more easily than you ever thought possible.

Before we talk about what makes up a character in Satori, I want to share another tool that can give you a huge boost in making swift, powerful change. That tool is to use an existing cultural hero-model to emulate. For me, it's often the idea of being a Jedi. I have a t-shirt with the Jedi Order symbol on it that I wear around town, and some patches with the same symbol that I have on other clothes. When I'm wearing this clothing, it's a constant reminder. Just putting on my shirt helps me become more aware, remember to be of service to others, exercise and practice my martial arts more. It's a simple way to inspire myself. You can do the same thing with clothing, pictures, objects, or even just *thinking* of yourself as a Jedi, a Forest Monk, a paladin, a mage, or whatever you like. In fact, what we're doing in this book is creating a hero-model of a Satorian for you. If you choose, you'll be able to adopt that as your hero-model, and use that as inspiration to stay strong on the path of solving Satori. This is all about the question often asked in social circles: What do you do? Bob might say "I'm a plumber", and that defines a lot about who he thinks he is. What would happen if you used that same power, but instead of defining yourself as a plumber/mechanic/whatever, defined yourself as a Jedi or Satorian?

How we define ourselves is further affected by what others think of us, or more aptly, what we *imagine* they think of us. But we'll learn more about that in Chapter 15 when we discuss NPCs (non-player characters).

Okay, let's dissect what a character is in Satori. Right now, your character has a set of attribute scores, tools, and skills. And just like in RPGs, Satori rewards you as you build your scores and gain new skills. As you know, every game has a different way to break down these character elements, so let's see how it works in Satori.

Attributes – *These are your basic attributes of fitness, charisma, discipline, resilience and knowledge.*

Virtues – *This is sort of like the modern, Western interpretation of karma.*

Awareness – *This is your ability to be aware of what is actually going on in Satori, rather than being deluded by distractions.*

Wisdom – *This is your ability to integrate what you gain by your awareness attribute, and apply it toward solving Satori.*

Understanding these essential elements of your character will allow you to focus your energies toward solving Satori. In the next chapter, let's dig in.

Morgan Speaks – *The character we became in Satori was not randomly generated. It was created specifically to deliver a high level of challenge for you. Remember that we can build our attributes, but that high attributes can also lead us into distractions. If someone is super ripped, it's easy for them to become obsessed with their own body. If someone is super hot, it's easy for them to get endlessly distracted in the attention their looks get them. So if your scores seem low, don't take that as a bad thing. Instead, see those places as opportunities to discover how building attributes leads us ever closer to solving Satori.*

---

chapter thirteen

BREAKING DOWN YOUR CHARACTER'S ATTRIBUTES

Let's look at those attributes. **Fitness** is the first one, and in Satori, it covers your raw muscular strength, agility, endurance, balance, health, and all other aspects of physical fitness. Some of us might have a resistance to building up our fitness, especially if we consider ourselves more intelligence-based. And it's true that to be successful in Satori, you don't have to have the strength of Conan or the agility of an Olympic gymnast. But every bit of fitness you add to your character is useful. Remember how the Jedi are more able to help others because they train physically? It's no different with your character. With additional fitness you'll be able to run away from the stray vicious dog and avoid some time in the hospital (although if you do end up in the ER, remember to use it as a clue!). You'll be able to catch the elderly woman who stumbles next to you (enhancing your Virtue, which we'll explain soon). And you'll find that you're more able to lend a hand, run to get help, and do all sorts of things that others may not be capable of.

I found an interesting example when my family went adventuring in Hawai'i for seven months. We loved coconuts, but it took a lot of strength to husk them. A machete did half the job, but the other half took a lot of back, arm, and grip strength. Luckily, I have been cultivating that sort of strength my whole life, and was able to husk endless coconuts to feed my family. Without that strength, I would have been extremely frustrated, and my family would have been pretty hungry. That hunger could have been a powerful distraction, preventing us from discovering many of the clues we discovered during our Hawai'i explorations.

There are many ways to build fitness, but the key is to find something fun and inspiring. It may be parkour or martial arts or backpacking or rock climbing. Find your fun, and your fun will inspire you to eat better, move more, and develop a higher fitness attribute.

Next is **charisma**. This is not about how sexy we look. In fact, physical attractiveness has little to do with charisma. Charisma is our ability to use our appearance, body language, and words in order to "open doors" with people. Because every person we meet in Satori has something to teach us, building up your charisma is essential. It makes the difference between an important clue-holding person brushing you off (and the clue being lost), and you being able to get the clue out of them. We'll talk about this more in the chapter on NPCs, but for now you can simply think of charisma as how well you can access the clues in the people all around you. Dale Carnegie's classic *How to Win Friends and Influence People* is perhaps the best textbook you can read on how to increase your charisma.

Discipline is made up of two elements – willpower and surrender. The surrender half of things is a transformation in discipline that happens further down the road of our journey, but in the meantime, willpower is what we're talking about. And your discipline is what makes the difference between things like movies, TV, or video games being clues rather than distractions. A low discipline will virtually guarantee that most of the game elements you encounter, from other people to daily situations to new TV series, will distract you into being ever-more-lost in the endless traps Satori sets before us. A high discipline will allow you to start to shift at least some of those elements so that you're able to see through the distractions to the clues hiding within them.

To build up discipline, we have to increase the strength of our willpower. Here's a crash course. To understand how to increase its strength, we can think of it like a magical pitcherful of willpower juice. The pitcher slowly refills due to its magic, but every time you do something that requires willpower, you have to pour some willpower juice out of the pitcher. Resist something small, and you'll pour out a little juice. Try to stop a major habit cold-turkey, and you'll pour out a lot. Empty the pitcher, and you'll break and fall prey to whatever you were resisting. AND, you'll slow down the magic of the pitcher so that it refills a little more slowly.

However, if you resist things but don't drain the pitcher, its rate of refill slowly increases.

It's as simple as that. The key is to use willpower every day, but to never drain the pitcher. Keep this balance, and you'll continually increase your refill rate until it refills so quickly that you can resist almost anything without danger of draining your pitcher. Just heed the warning not to drain your pitcher. Always keep it at least half full, but make sure to drain something from the pitcher each day.

One fun way to do this is the Bowl of Challenges. To make this, get a bowl or bag, and many small pieces of paper. On each piece of paper, write down a challenge. One might be to call someone you haven't called in over a year. Another might be to try a new food today. Yet another might be to sleep outside tonight. Make most of them simple challenges, but add a few (like that outside overnight) that are a little tougher. Create at least twenty or thirty of these, and then, once a day, reach into the bowl and pull one out. Hold yourself 100% to completing the challenge. Doing this will not only build willpower, but will also encourage you to break out of habitual gameplay patterns and encourage new clues to emerge in your game.

Resilience is next. This is your ability to "bounce back" from situations that affect you emotionally, or to deal with stress. If a person with low resilience is driving to work and someone flips them off, they will stew about it all day long, allowing that simple finger gesture to stir up their emotions, get them down, and maybe launch them into a tirade about how screwed up the world is. A person with high resilience, however, won't be affected by that finger gesture at all, perhaps just taking the time to smile from the heart and send the finger-flipper some love and compassion.

The bad news is that resilience is one of the toughest attributes to build up. One reason for this is that our distractions, in the form of movies and other entertainment, often glorify or showcase people with low resilience (think *drama).* The good news is that resilience naturally increases the more you journey forward in Satori. The ReWild University YouTube channel is filled with videos that teach how to develop resilience, so feel free to use them to your advantage. But know that every step of the way along the game of Satori (as long as you are busy uncovering clues rather than getting lost in distractions), you'll gain in resilience. If you want a boost to this attribute, observe where you can choose challenge over comfort. Will you take a nice long hot shower in the morning, or an ice cold one? Sit on the couch to watch a movie, or stretch and do some yoga while you watch? Refuse to eat the offal stew your grandma made, or grin and bear it?

The last attribute, **knowledge**, is a double-edged sword. It's celebrated within the game of Satori as one of the most important things we can gain, and yet the truth is that knowledge sets a very devious trap for us.

Notice that knowledge divides the world. Think of a grade-school kid in their first anatomy class. Up until now, he's thought of the human body as one whole thing. But now he's taught that it is actually composed of all sorts of parts. There is a heart, a liver, lungs, eyeballs, bones, and a tongue. And for most of us, that's where the knowledge ends. For the rest of our lives we think of the body as composed of all sorts of different objects put together, much like a machine. And the game of Satori (as it does with many things) gives superficial evidence that this view is true. After all, we can remove a person's heart and put in a mechanical one, right? Clearly, the body is a bunch of stitched together parts.

However, if knowledge of the body is pursued further, we start to learn that there isn't a clear line between one organ and the next. The liver, for instance, is tied in intimately with the actions of the gall bladder and the blood, which is tied in intimately with the heart. The closer we look at an organ's actions and "boundaries", the more we find that drawing a clear line isn't so easy. Eventually, a picture of interconnection and oneness begins to develop, and that is where wisdom begins to blossom.

This is perhaps most easily seen in a simple exercise one can do with a piece of paper and a pencil. If you have some handy, give it a try. Put down the book, and draw a tree. Then read on.

If you did the exercise (and you're like most people), you drew a line across the paper to represent the ground, and then drew a trunk, some branches, and leaves. In other words, we usually draw what we see, or what is most easily accessible to our knowledge. Some people will have gone a bit deeper and drawn roots, realizing that without those roots, the tree clearly cannot exist. But even with roots, we're still using a very superficial brand of knowledge. Learn more about trees, and we'll discover that they depend completely on the soil (granted, it may be difficult to draw soil). And that the microbes and fungi in the soil are woven in with the roots and also 100% vital to the tree's ability to be a tree. We can't stop there, because we need to draw the sun, and we also need water. Continue learning more and more about a tree's life, and we'll soon see that it is interconnected through a never-ending web to everything else in the Satori universe (quick geeky note for coders -- this is also one of the secrets to how the game was "programmed", because programming shifted from trying to input endless details to programming "oneness", which naturally blossoms into apparent details).

If we are taught only superficial knowledge, we receive a picture of a universe composed of many "things", all trying to eke out their existence amongst each other. But if we delve deeper into that knowledge, we begin to see that things are much more connected than we ever imagined.

To build your knowledge attribute, you have to get into the habit of not "stopping" in your learning. If something teaches divisions, keep searching and exploring until you find someone who can explain how things eventually become un-divided again. Basic physics will divide the world into objects that obey certain unbreakable laws. Quantum physics will turn that idea on its head, leading us into a non-intuitive understanding of the world where solid things are made up of mostly-empty space and the building-blocks of the world exist only in a state of probability rather than certainty.

This is an essential understanding in the game of Satori, and it goes beyond knowledge. Look on the surface of things, and the game will present you with a reality that seems to make perfect sense but that is actually just a trap to lead you ever deeper into being tangled in illusion. We'll talk more about this when we discuss wisdom in a few chapters. For now, simply understand that knowledge, if followed just as far as usually presented, will lead to illusion. But if followed far enough, it leads to clues, and those lead to wisdom.

Satori will feed your mind with knowledge from many sources -- media, friends, parents, religious figures, documentaries, and people with various ideas about the world. This knowledge is useful within the game dynamics, but none of it, unless it leads you to wisdom, brings you any closer to solving Satori. Everything covered by "conspiracy theories", politics, "news" and even science is only distraction unless it leads you toward wisdom.

Note that as we move forward and talk about virtues, awareness, and wisdom, that we might question why these things are not simple attributes like the ones we've just covered. Well, we could certainly put them in that group, but these three are so deep and essential that virtues will have their own chapter, we'll hit awareness in Chapter Seventeen, and talk more about wisdom in Chapter Eighteen.

DM Speaks – *As a character, it is essential to build yourself up even as you tear yourself down. Do not let your attributes define you. They are there only to lead you ever closer to me, your true nature. Then, you must let them go. So pick them up and use them as you would use a boat and oars to cross a river, but once you gain the other side, it is time to let the current take the boat away, for they are not who you truly are.*

chapter fourteen
VIRTUES

Seriously? Virtues? This isn't Sunday school, after all. Why are we talking about being kind, loving, and compassionate?

The 1985 video game *Ultima IV* was revolutionary, primarily because it broke the mold of "hero must save the world from the evil one" and introduced a new, deeper gameplay. Interestingly, it focused on virtues, and your behavior in the game determined your chances of success. In this way, *Ultima IV* was actually an inspiration for Satori's gameplay.

We get another insight into virtues from the Star Wars universe, where Force-sensitive individuals must choose between the light side and the dark side. And often, the dark side is presented as more powerful, with the light side being limited by their reluctance to kill, get angry, or manipulate people. In many other movies and stories, evil is also presented as immensely powerful, and even in the Satori gameplay, we often see evil holding the upper hand (especially as presented on the evening news with endless stories of murder, shootings, bombings, and more).

However, in reality, the dark side is incredibly limited, as was explained earlier by Cowan. Because it is self-serving, it requires the wielder to be lost in the illusion of the Little Me, and the Little Me simply cannot access the deeper powers Satori offers. It limits itself by its own beliefs. Yes, the Little Me can be loud, it can be violent, and it can do a lot of damage. But its powers are always limited and held in check by Satori. The most we'll get by being evil is to build up our Little Me and join the ranks of the deluded and lost.

Virtues are so powerful because far from just being ways to be "nice", each one helps us to distance ourselves from the Little Me and come closer and closer to our DM nature. After all, the most powerful players in Satori are not concerned with themselves. Their Little Me has mostly dissolved, and their new "me" has become so big and all-encompassing that it cannot be harmed by anything, including "death". In fact, when someone at this level of Satori game play dies within the game, they have probably just "leveled up" to opening new dimensions of play not available to most of us.

And remember, when it comes to cultivating virtues, it doesn't matter what you've done in the past. You can start over NOW. Reinvent yourself NOW. You are not defined by your memories. THIS is the moment to leave behind the petty desires of the Little Me and move forward toward your true self and true power.

Let's look at the virtues in Satori, and how each one will guide you closer toward solving the game.

Compassion is first. Often, we define compassion as feeling sorry for people, but this isn't compassion at all. Note that in feeling sorry for someone, we separate ourselves from them, looking in at their situation and then making ourselves feel a little less guilty for our fortune by feeling sorry for their misfortune.

Instead, compassion is more like putting yourself in another's shoes. Sometimes we can do this almost literally. If someone is stuck in the mud, the compassionate person doesn't stand outside the mud-puddle and tell them how bad they feel for them. Instead, they get right in there themselves, take the person's hand, and then, together and strengthened by companionship, the two make their way out. But often we can't do this physically, and have to do it in our minds. If someone has lost a person they love, we can use our imagination to put ourselves in their place, and in that way we can feel at least a tiny fraction of what they are feeling. We do our best to come to their place, and relate to them more intimately.

Compassion is all about intimacy – coming as close as we can to others, both in actual situations, and in our imaginations. By doing so, we build connection with the people around us, but we also take the focus away from ourselves and onto others. In doing so, we accomplish two things. First, we create more happiness and joy for ourselves in the game, because doing things for others actually brings more happiness than doing things for ourselves. But secondly, we take energy away from the Little Me, who identifies only with our little bag of flesh, and put energy toward discovering a larger, more interconnected me, which leads us toward discovering how we have DM nature inside of us. Every time we act in compassion, we come closer to solving Satori. Every time we condemn, judge, or think ourselves wiser/smarter/better than someone else, we're actually engaging in self-sabotage, entrenching ourselves deeper into the Little Me and Satori's illusions.

The second virtue in Satori is **curiosity**. Curiosity also reverses our usual tendency to judge, because it's the opposite of judgment. If you see a person and judge them not worth talking to, you close a door. Whatever clues they held for you are lost. Satori always offers us the opportunity to sabotage ourselves or lead ourselves astray, and judgment is one of the most powerful ways it leads us away from solving its mysteries.

Curiosity, however, opens doors. It looks at that

person and instead of judging them, gets curious about them. Curiosity takes courage – fear judges, because then it can hide behind its judgment and not have to confront anything except its own closed mind. Get curious, and things get scary. We have to approach that person who might be intimidating, or attractive, or strange looking. We have to get up the courage to talk with them, to try to find an entrance into their world and discover whatever clues they hold for us (more about this in Chapter 15).

By now you may be noticing a pattern in Satori. In the game, our Little Me minds are conditioned into certain set behaviors (for instance, to judge situations rather than be curious). But those "default" behavior patterns are actually the *opposite* of what's needed to solve Satori. You can see how it works. The superficial, everyday signs always point in the wrong direction. We have to question the status quo, the cultural mores, the "common sense" views of the world which few take the time to question.

With curiosity, we again begin to erode our attachment to the Little Me. Little Me depends on judgment to keep it safe. If we explore the world with curiosity, we are guaranteed to begin to see through the matrix, to notice that judgment closes us to learning any new clues. Curiosity begins to move us out of our small boxes and see the world in a more complete way. And that, my fellow Satorians, takes us forward on the journey.

Love is the most powerful of all the virtues, and also one of the least understood. Too often, the word "love" is equated with the sort of relationships we see in most marriages. It doesn't take too much observation to see that most marriages are really a sort of ownership, where people consider the other person to be "theirs". We see this in most parent/child relationships as well, where "love" is a sort of control. These are tragic manifestations of the deep but hidden frustration most of us feel, a powerlessness that we can only relieve by "owning" another person or exerting control over a child.

Love, however, is not ownership, nor is it control. Instead, love is a complete surrender of our self-ness, the dissolving of the Little Me, as we give ourselves completely, without restriction or condition.

To our Little Me mind, this sounds like a very bad idea, as if we should just love people and do whatever they tell us, and be used and abused by everyone we encounter.

Well, we can assure the Little Me that the situation is a bit different than that. Love does NOT mean giving ourselves away through our actions, or allowing others to boss us around, control us, or abuse us. In fact, love has little to do with actions at all, but rather an inner state. To gain the virtue of love, we must open our hearts in a non-judging way and love those we encounter unconditionally, without any need for them to have merit, to do what we want, or even to be nice to us. As we nurture that love, it will naturally result in us being curious about them, and that curiosity combined with love automatically invokes compassion.

Do you see how this works? Love is feeling-based, not action-based. If we use the example of someone who is bothering us, like a boss who treats us unfairly, we simply look at them and feel the love emerging from our hearts. That will break us free of judgment (what a jerk!), and instead invoke curiosity (I wonder why he's so mean to the people who work for him? What inside of him is hurting so badly that he feels compelled to lash out at others?). That will in turn lead us to compassion (trying to imagine ourselves in a place of hurt that is so profound that we would willingly harm those around us). Now we are in his shoes, and can see him as a teacher and fellow player in the game, lost and afraid and possibly in need of a helping hand. At this point we may attempt to reach out to him. If that is unsuccessful, and we are being hurt too much working for him, it may very well be time to leave the job and let him continue on his own journey. We are NOT called to be his savior or his punching bag. But in being guided by love/curiosity/compassion, we have a chance of breaking through to him, and uncovering the clues he holds for us (because he does indeed hold clues).

Always, with love, we must be aware of how much energy we use in remaining in a situation. Hurt is a major energy drain, and we won't be able to concentrate on the overall gameplay if we are hurting endlessly trying to uncover a few clues from one person or situation. Thus, it doesn't pay to stay in a situation or relationship if it is just bringing us pain. However, as we nurture love in our lives, we will find that the game stops giving us so many hurtful situations, and that when we do receive one, it is usually transformed quickly through application of our virtues.

The final virtue is **service**. Through this virtue, we step into someone's life and help them in some way. It doesn't take much to see what a door-opener this is. Shovel the sidewalk of the grumpy lady next door, and a few weeks from now you might be sitting down to cookies and tea and hearing an important clue. Buy lunch for a homeless vet, and some important clues will be delivered over the lunchtime conversation. Stop and help someone with their flat tire, and more clues are waiting.

There is a caveat with service, and that is to remember to be wary of committing to long-term service. Unless our virtue of love is especially strong, too much service will begin to build resentment inside of us. The more love you have, the more service you will be capable of, but in the beginning, keep your service short-term. Also, be aware of the Little Me tendency to "count points", where we quietly keep tab in our minds of how much we've done for someone (and usually, how little they have done in return). This is the killer of marriages, the builder of resentment, and the destroyer of our virtues. Comparisons of any kind entrench us in the Little Me and all the endless suffering that involves.

Do you see how virtues work? They are door-openers, allowing us to see past the superficial offerings of Satori, get glimpses through the matrix, and begin to unearth clues in the people and situations around us.

If we embrace Little Me thinking (often equated with the word "evil" in our world), we will see only our own illusions, and be forever lost in the game, a puppet and slave. As we embrace virtues, we take the helm and begin to guide our own gameplay. The game gives us better things and situations, and becomes a lot more fun. And we make continued progress toward solving Satori and discovering the ultimate treasure awaiting all who can solve the final puzzle.

We can use virtues independently, making a conscious effort to be curious or compassionate, or we can utilize the natural flow of the virtues, in the one direction following the flow of love to curiosity to compassion, and in the other direction following the flow of compassion to curiosity to love to service.

Want an easy-to-use exercise that will help you develop these virtues, plus give you access to one of Satori's best-kept secrets?

GLOW Meditation

The early morning, when you first wake up and are awake but not awake, is a special time. It is called "The Time of Nectar". This special moment of the day is when our minds are most open to conditioning. Wake up to a harsh alarm clock and rush to work, and your day will likely feel rushed. Wake up to the rising sun and a morning meditation, and your day will be filled with wonders. The GLOW meditation helps you accomplish this.

When you wake up, stay relaxed, and go through your GLOW.

Gratitude -- Think of something or someone you're grateful for. Really FEEL the gratitude. And then let the something or someone go, and just dwell in the feeling for as long as you wish. Then, move to Love.

Love -- Think of something or someone you love. Sink into the feeling. Then let go of the person you are thinking of, and just dwell in love for as long as you wish. Then move to Oneness.

Oneness -- This one will evolve for you as you continue on your journey. The idea is to soak into whatever concept of oneness makes sense to you right now. Feel as connected with the world as you can in whatever way feels best. Then move on to Wonder.

Wonder -- It's time to wake up more fully, but before

you do, ask yourself "I wonder what amazing, magical things I'll discover today?" Feel that sense of curiosity. This will set you on the route to being curious rather than judgmental as you encounter your day, and the incantation holds a bit of magic as well. In fact, this is the secret I referred to earlier. You may find that when you use those words, oddly incredible things do indeed appear in your life. Pay attention to what wonders you experience as they unfold in the day before you.

Take as much time as you want with GLOW. You can take ten seconds in each portion, or ten minutes. The important part is "feeling" each portion as deeply as you can.

Cowan Faol Speaks – *We can imagine life as two banks of a river, with rushing water between them. Most people dwell on one side, where life is confusing, often desperate, and filled with frustrations and anxieties. On the other side is Nirvana, Shambala, the Garden of Eden. But to get to the other side, we need stepping-stones, and those stepping-stones are the virtues. As each virtue serves to loosen the Little Me's hold on us, we take step after step across the stones. Once on the other side, we can help others to join us. But without those stepping stones, we are confined to the muddy, messy bank where everyone struggles. Use the virtues wisely, my friend. They are our most powerful tools to unconvince us that we're the Little Me, and begin to reveal the truth – that you are DM.*

chapter fifteen
NPCs

We've been talking about ourselves a lot – the Little Me and the pre-programming that keeps us deluded. But what about other people? What's going on with our family, friends, and peers? If you are actually a DM hiding from itself, are they too?

Well, to answer those questions, we have to go deep. Ready? Let's dive in.

In RPGs, the people you interact with basically come in two types. There are player characters, who are played by real people, and NPCs, who are played by the DM or the computer.

In your memory, you can probably recall how computer NPCs have become more and more intelligent and realistic. As AI increases in potency, you'll see them become even more realistic. By the time Satori comes around, NPCs will be indistinguishable (to most eyes) from player characters.

As you look around you in Satori, who is who? Is everyone a player character? Or are some (or most, or all) people NPCs?

The answer (confusingly) is that everyone is both. I know. Paradoxical. But such is the genius behind Satori. To understand this is impossible for our rational, Little Me minds, but will make perfect sense as we move into the participatory mindset.

To begin to unravel this puzzle of Satori, we have to go through a number of different perspectives. First, let's think of Satori as a purely subjective, perception-based game, with you as the player character and everyone else you interact with as NPCs. Let's run with this, but remember that we are back in the realm of myth, outlining a method of thinking that is simultaneously true and untrue.

In this subjective view of Satori, you have been brought into the game just a short while ago, implanted with memories so that you believe you've been alive for all the moments that led up until this one. Your mind is pre-programmed to pay attention to all the wrong things, and to believe that you "win" the game through the exact opposite actions that will actually help you solve Satori. As the only player character in your game, you are surrounded by NPCs. These are friends, colleagues, garbage collectors, homeless people, politicians, movie stars, family members, and pet dogs. And ALL of these NPCs are put into your game for specific reasons. NONE of them are there arbitrarily. Every one of them holds one or more clues for you. None of them come into your gameplay without holding the potential to guide you toward solving Satori.

NPCs are like a book. They hold stories, ideas, clues, and traps, but most of these books are locked. To open those locks, we have to use a little magic, and conjure a key that fits. Each person requires a different incantation, gestures, and reagents to successfully conjure the key. The garbage collector wearing a Green Bay Packers shirt might require you to lean up against the garbage truck and ask him what he thought about last night's football game. Only then will you pique his interest, at which point he'll start to open up and perhaps offer a clue. Your college professor might require you to visit her office and share with her how you're having a tough time in class because you're addicted to video games and can't seem to devote enough time to studying. Only then will she step out of the professor role and offer up her clue. And a co-worker who is always the butt of others' jokes might share life-changing wisdom with you when you give her some sincere and friendly connection.

In general, NPCs are all busy going about their own lives, and the clues they hold won't be available to you.

They'll either pass you by as just another stranger, or if they are someone you know and interact with, they will show only a small part of themselves, as if you are seeing only the cover of their book.

To gain clues from NPCs, we have to somehow break them out of their programmed role. Sometimes this is easy. Sometimes it will seem impossible. But we won't get much of anywhere in Satori unless we start to see NPCs as our teachers. Virtues are the big door openers, helping to break people from their programmed role and open them up.

Now, you've probably been pre-programmed with more than a little social anxiety, so this idea of engaging creatively with people might be pretty intimidating. But seeing others as NPCs can help. Before, people were "real people", and often intimidating. We're afraid of what they'll think of us, if they'll brush us off, tease us, or kick our asses. But now we see that people are something completely different – each one is a puzzle, and if we are savvy and wise (and use our virtues), we can open their locks and discover what is inside.

Now, I said that ALL the NPCs you encounter are in your game for a reason, right? I have to qualify that a bit. Because if you walk down the streets of New York City, you're going to see a LOT of people. Is each one of these put into your game on purpose, and you're supposed to somehow connect with all nine million of them?

Of course not. Many of these are just background, just placed in your world as details to make the Satori gameplay more immersive. But all of them do hold clues for us (everything in Satori gameplay does). And some of them are going to stand out from the crowd, and those are the ones that we need to pay attention to. In Hawai'i as I wrote this, there was a man who rode his bike up the hill near our home every day. He was recurrent, so I knew he had a clue for me. While walking down the sidewalk in NYC, you might see someone who looks very attractive to you. That's a sign. In a classroom of otherwise unremarkable people, one person might give you a mean look. That's the person who has entered your gameplay and holds a clue for you. Basically, if you take notice of someone, for whatever reason, they are a more active NPC in your game. Just like in a "game-within-the-game" like *Assassin's Creed,* those NPCs are important parts of your gameplay.

What if you're too scared, and let that attractive person walk by, or you are too intimidated to try to open the book of that person who gave you a mean look in class? That's okay. Satori gives you lots of chances. If you let some slip by, odds are the same clue will come again in the guise of another NPC. And sometimes, the clue a person holds doesn't require you to talk with them. Sometimes the clue is in *your reaction* to their appearance in your game.

So in general, you'll get second and third and fourth chances to receive clues. In Satori, this is called "clue recurrence". This means that the same clue will come into your gameplay again and again in different guises until you "get it". But sometimes, when Satori throws in a major clue, it will only come once. This book is one of them. Put this book aside, and you may never get a clue that is this revealing again. It doesn't mean you can't solve Satori without this book. All the clues contained in it will be revealed in other ways, through different NPCs, situations, and experiences. But if you set aside this book, it may take years or decades for all of the clues it contains to be revealed in other forms. Rest assured that Satori will always make these major clues very obvious. They will be found in things that really jump out at you. Some may be revealed in the form of an NPC who speaks a few powerful, life-changing words and then goes on their way, never to be seen again. Some might come in the form of a YouTube video that strikes you to the soul. Another might be the person you fall in love with, who will reveal clue after clue for as long as you're together.

Okay, so what about that confusing part about everyone being both NPCs and player characters? Well, as I said, our Little Me won't be able to wrap its head around this, but we can at least draw a rough picture to give us a pointer.

Let's begin with those NPCs. They are also player

characters. Every one that you perceive (yes, even all of those that you see walk by on the sidewalk of NYC) is a player character, each one of them is DM, each one of them is someone like Morgan, playing a game in which they've forgotten who they really are. Each one has been given a new body, mind, and memories, and their ultimate goal is to solve the game by using clues, to enter the participatory mindset, and to eventually discover who they really are.

How can they be both player characters and NPCs? The easiest way for the Little Me mind to think of it is to imagine that when someone is deluded by the Little Me and the non-participatory mindset, their character is basically controlled by the pre-programming in the game. They *think* they are in control of their thoughts, opinions, and actions, but someone else has decided that they are Libertarians, love fantasy RPGs, are fans of Star Wars, and truly want to own a real-life lightsaber. In other words, we might replace the term "non-player character" with the term "non-participatory character". A non-participatory character is lost in the game, unaware that they are playing, and basically acting on autopilot. But each one, just like ourselves, has the potential to transform into a PC, a participatory character.

Yes. Just like ourselves. Because not only is everyone *else* simultaneously NPCs and PCs, but you are too. When your Little Me is in control, you are being run primarily on autopilot. The "choices" you make are not yours, even though they might feel like it. The person you are crushing on, the philosophies you espouse, the programs you like to watch – these are all just pre-programming, determined by forces outside of you. You are "lost" in the game. Remember, it doesn't matter if you're a rock star or a struggling artist -- even "successful" people can be lost. Most are.

NPCs only become player characters when they begin to unravel clues, enter the participatory mindset, and begin to leave the Little Me behind. Slowly, they are given more and more control over their own actions and over the environment around them. Only then do we realize that the apparent control we thought we had as the Little Me was an illusion. Only then do we move past being slaves and begin the journey into something infinitely more.

The concept of NPCs, then, has a single essential thing to give us. That is, that in every NPC we encounter, there is a player character hidden inside of them. If you like, you can help them to bring that player character out (in fact, doing so will sometimes aid us in our own journeys, though we can easily get lost in thinking of ourselves as gurus). This is similar to the Hindu "namaste", in which we greet other people in a way that acknowledges the God-nature dwelling inside each of us. We don't say "namaste" just to the person standing in front of us, but to the DM inside of them and acting through them.

To further make the idea of NPCs confusing, I want to bring in one more huge clue – another myth that can help us solve Satori. Consider that in addition to everything else you've read so far, we could also see that DM, the creator of Satori, is playing ALL the characters in Satori. DM created its own game, entered the game and forgot itself, becoming Morgan and countless other players all at once, all dwelling in their regular lives and hiding from their own true nature through distractions. Some of those characters sat down and created Satori, a game within DM's game, and then Morgan and countless others signed up for Satori and started playing, also forgetting themselves and becoming you and all the people you perceive around you. You're the third layer, believing you are you, just a bag of flesh, while in reality you are DM, playing three levels away from your actual, true nature.

Perplexed? As we go deeper into Satori's gameplay it's easy to get lost in the rabbit hole. Sometimes it can feel like it would be nice if we could just have our own personal Morpheus. If NPCs hold clues, is it possible that some are gurus or wise figures who will guide us in the right direction? After all, stories and games almost always feature such NPCs. Think Gandalf. Think Yoda. Are they present in Satori?

They are, but be careful. Most such "gurus" are there to lead you astray. Like much entertainment and media, they are elements of the game that seem interesting, but are really just distractions. No matter how wise a would-be Morpheus seems to you, make sure that you think for yourself. In no case will Satori give you someone who will tell you exactly how to solve the game. That's too easy, and requires very little on your part. A good Morpheus will help you learn to think for yourself, to explore clues without giving you answers. And most of all, a true Morpheus will radiate love from their eyes. They will be genuinely concerned about you, and you'll be able to feel that in the way they treat you. If someone is claiming to be a Morpheus but is mistreating you, then you know they are not what they seem. Do not doubt your own wisdom, and do not follow someone else's path. Each route to solving Satori is unique to each player. There is no "one right way". One fun part of the game, however, is finding others who are active player characters -- in other words, others who know they are players in this game. They may be few and far between, but as you begin to play more consciously, you'll find more and more people who "see behind the scenes" of the matrix.

If any of this is feeling utterly confusing, don't worry. By the end of the book, or at worst, a couple of years from now when you read this book again, things will make sense in new ways. Anything that is too confusing can just be left behind right now. It will percolate in your mind and slowly cook.

Once we understand that Satori surrounds us with NPCs, each of whom holds clues and each of whom can help us to break free of our Little Me illusion (and each of whom we in turn can help to break free of *their* Little Me illusion), we'll once again see how virtues come into play. Without the mindset afforded by the virtues, we'll be too wrapped up in our Little Me to look people in the eyes and see DM looking back.

When we start to see DM in others, we simultaneously help them in their own gameplay, and we start to see through the veil to encounter DM and the powerful clues DM gives us. Since we've been speaking of clues so much lately, it's probably time to delve in and see just what clues are.

Cowan Faol Speaks – *As humans, we can get pretty human-centric. Yes, NPCs hold incredible clues, but so do all the other elements of the world that DM is becoming. When we treat people with love and compassion, they will open up to us in amazing ways. And the same goes for trees, spiders, the wind, and all the other elements of nature. Treat these things well, and each one has the potential to lead us to our true state of being. Treat them badly, and doors will close. This goes for individual creatures (makes you think twice about whether you are going to squash that spider in your room or instead do a catch-and-release), and for the overall way in which we treat the world (in the parlance of your world, how "green" you live). Treat the world well enough, and it starts to become "alive" and will provide you with all sorts of perks in the game. When I created the world of Elorien, I entered a deep relationship with every element of the world. The first effect I noticed was that after about a year, the world began to "become friends" with me by giving me things that made my gameplay incredibly fun and enjoyable. The second effect I noticed is that it led me even deeper into my DM nature. DM is all of the things we see around us, and as we "fall in love" with everything, we lose ourselves into our DM nature. When you and I realize our full DM nature, we will be able to simultaneously be everything and everywhen (Kenton will talk more about this in Chapter Twenty-Two). So just as we treat other people (who are really ourselves) with compassion and love, and thus break down the barriers between ourselves and others, when we treat the world with compassion and love, we break down the perceived barriers between ourselves and that spider crawling across the kitchen floor. We start to become All.*

chapter sixteen
CLUES

In RPGs, clues are usually fairly straightforward. In *Ultima IV*, one NPC tells us to find another NPC named Pepper, who will tell us where the Rune of Compassion is hidden. The situation is similar in Satori, except the clues come in various types, and not all are so easy to follow. They are not just requesting us to perform actions, but are woven into our thoughts, experiences, emotions, and memories. They are extremely sophisticated, often subtle, and most are paired with distractions that will turn your gaze away from them. In this chapter we'll come to understand different clue types, and how to use them wisely.

But first let's go back to the time before we realized something was "going on"; before we realized we were playing Satori. At that point, we were completely lost in

Satori and everything seemed to just happen randomly. Many players won't advance past this stage, because they are so convinced that the universe is senseless and meaningless. The world holds no clues, but just random experiences that jumble together, and the best we can do is try to piece things together enough so that we can enjoy the most distractions possible until we die. "Successful" people will obtain a lot of distractions (followers, a huge house, money to manage, etc.), but they will be no less anxious, fearful, or confused than anyone else. As I mentioned before, it doesn't really matter how much stuff you accumulate in Satori. You don't win or get any real advantages by being in the "1%". Becoming royalty or a movie star or the president will only tend to get a person more lost in the game. None of these accomplishments will do you any good while you're stuck in Satori (which explains why celebrities are so often abusing drugs, a third of lawyers drink too much, and in the U.S., we lose a doctor a day to suicide).

"Success" in Satori isn't success as people usually think of it. Success in Satori comes from understanding the basics of the game, which are like an ultra-elaborate game of hide-and-seek in which you've agreed to become so immersed in another persona that you completely forget who you are. Then, to make it unbelievably challenging, the game sets up a gameplay where your "gaze" is deliberately and constantly turned in the wrong directions. But scattered into the gameplay are clues – people, experiences, videos, books, and other elements of the game where, in various ways, your gaze is pointed in the right direction.

The first class of clues are of the type most familiar to us.

In-game Clues – *Clues where one element of the game (a person, book, etc.) points you to another element of the game where further clues await.*

You're walking down the street on a windy day when a piece of paper tumbles across the pavement and rests writing-side up on the sidewalk in front of you. It says: "The Non-Dual Society meets this Wednesday at the library at 3 o'clock sharp. Don't come, because you can't". You've just been given an in-game clue. Likely, if you go to the meeting, you're going to meet someone, hear something, or be given a book recommendation that will move you forward in your quest to solve Satori.

Because in-game clues lead from one element of the game to another (one person, place, or situation to another), our various attributes will be called into service. The next clue might be at the top of a cliff or under twenty feet of water. It might be locked away deep in conversation with an intimidating-looking body-builder, or in the words of a child. The more you've developed your attributes, the more you'll be able to wiggle clues out of people, situations, or places.

Usually, in-game clues will simply point you in the direction of other people, places, or situations that will guide you forward, though sometimes they will lead to a synchronicity or realization clue, which we'll discuss shortly.

Before we hit those two important types of clues, I want to mention atmospheric clues, which are usually extremely subtle.

Atmospheric Clues – *Akin to the Japanese concept of wabi sabi, these clues consist of moments when you see "mistakes" that are intentionally put in Satori in order to give us a chance to notice that the game is less "real" than we imagine it to be.*

Atmospheric clues come in two sub-types – environmental clues and memory clues. These clues are basically intentional mistakes or "artifacts" in the game. Environmental artifacts are places where you will see something that looks a little "fake". They can sometimes be seen in clouds, reflections, or in some other detail of the environment around you. Cities, which are filled with detail, will sometimes display these artifacts. The abnormally large moon that we sometimes see on the horizon is one – an artifact that is still not adequately explained by science, but seems to be a "glitch" in our perception or the way the world "renders" for us (which we'll learn more about in Chapter Twenty-Six).

The significance of these clues is to remind us that the world we are experiencing is not "real" in the way our Little Me mind thinks it is.

Some atmospheric clues are related to Synchronicity Clues (which we will discuss in a moment) but are synchronicities that anyone can experience, rather than personal things that happen in your life. You can think of these as billboards that DM puts in the game to say, "Hey, you could take this as just a big coincidence, but check this out – it's so fakey of a coincidence that it's actually a clue put here to tell you that this is all a big made-up game". One example is how Douglas Adams, the author of *The Hitchiker's Guide to the Galaxy,* described how the massive computer Deep Thought spent 7.5 million years pondering the answer to Life, the Universe, and Everything. The answer was 42. Decades later, Cambridge astronomers led by Dr. Richard Saunders announced that they had calculated the Hubble Constant, a measurement of how quickly objects in the universe are moving away from each other (which could help us calculate the age of the universe). What was the Hubble Constant? You guessed it. 42. (Km/s/Mpc, though we have since found that it varies depending on where you look in the universe, and the measurement keeps changing as we learn more and develop more accurate instruments.)

Another fun one? What is the longest word that you can spell in the English language that uses only the letters on the top row of a keyboard? Well, it's "typewriter".

Physicists encounter atmospheric clues in their work to unravel the nature of reality. From wave-particle duality to non-locality to the weird results of the famous double-slit experiment, physics is filled with atmospheric clues.

Finally, we have memory artifacts, a type of atmospheric clue that is essentially a "mistake" in the programming of our Little Me minds. These can be memories of childhood things, like the 90's movie *Shazaam*, the kids' classic about a genie, which you may remember but is now claimed to have never existed. Or you may remember the famous Star Wars line where Darth Vader says, "Luke, I am your father." Except again, you'll now find that he is claimed to have said, "No, I am your father."

More subtle are moments when you are hit with a sudden but vague memory of some other time in your life, when things were somehow more magical or pure. Again, there is a Japanese concept called yugen that is very similar. You might even seem to remember other lives, or have the feeling of half-remembering a time when you were very, very young and saw the world through completely different eyes. These clues aren't going to propel us forward on our journey in huge ways, but they are often the first hints we are given in the game that the world isn't quite what we think it is. If we have experienced enough of these clues, and have given them enough attention, they will sometimes trigger the beginning of synchronicity clues and realization clues.

Synchronicity Clues – *These are what most people call "coincidences", but the more we advance in our gameplay, the more we're able to consciously control coincidences and thus we discover that they are actually participatory.*

Synchronicity clues have the important purpose of slowly unconvincing us of our conviction that the world we see is "real", and governed by mindless laws of physics. As our journey progresses and we develop our attributes and virtues, we begin to enter the participatory mindset, and we'll have more and more of these clues enter our gameplay. At first our Little Me mind will dismiss them as coincidences. But as we gain more control over our gameplay and begin to see how life "lines up" according to our assumptions, beliefs, and ideas, the "coincidences" will become so ridiculous that it will be tough for the Little Me to convince us any more.

Rebecca and I had an example of a synchronicity clue when we were debating whether to purchase a juicer. I felt it was too expensive to justify, but she felt quite sure we needed one. We lived next to a pine forest, and in jest, I thought of the silliest thing I could think of to juice.

"What are we going to do with it? Juice pine needles?" I asked sarcastically.

We ended up purchasing the juicer. And as I read the instruction manual, I suddenly stopped, mouth agape. There in front of me were instructions for juicing — you guessed it — pine needles. As I mentioned, single instances like this are easy to dismiss as coincidence, but after the pine needle incident we experienced a flood of synchronicity clues that instilled the impression that there was something strange operating behind the scenes of reality.

Pay attention to these very direct clues, since a major part of gameplay involves re-conditioning your mind. The momentum of our Little Me mind and the non-participatory mindset are very powerful, and it can take hundreds of synchronicity clues to begin to shift our minds. It's a slow process, but it can be expedited if we give direct attention to these clues.

Finally, the most powerful and direct clues in the game. These clues are triggered by the other clue types, the development of our attributes and virtues, and how much we immerse ourselves in the details of the game.

Realization Clues – *Ranging from minor realizations of how our Little Me isn't as solid as we thought it was to full-blown "enlightenment experiences", these clues give us direct, wordless experiences of our true nature.*

Minor realization clues are often set in motion by our interactions with another person. These happen when someone's words or actions help us realize that an aspect of our Little Me isn't as "real" as we thought it was. An example might be when a co-worker is telling you what a jerk you are, and you suddenly switch from feeling offended to realizing that they aren't saying anything about you, but only about their own judgments. That can help you recognize your own judging mind, and in that recognition, your judging mind becomes a little weaker. It's a big step forward in your game when other people's judgments of you no longer offend you, but instead start to trigger these realizations. These clues can also be initiated by a person's kindness, by their indifference, or by an action that you witness them performing. Since other people are invariably one of the most powerful forces in our gameplay, our reactions to them are treasure chests filled with clues.

The other type of realization clues often hit us suddenly, infusing us with a feeling of unity, or giving us a wordless understanding of one of life's "big mysteries." For instance, you might be walking along a path and all of a sudden realize that even though you are walking, you aren't moving. In that moment, the true nature of space and time become completely clear, even though you can't attach any words to the clarity.

These "enlightenment experiences" may last only a few moments, or in some cases a few days, until they begin to fade. But each one will catapult you forward in the game. These come with their own dangers, as many people will have one or more of these experiences and then imagine they are "awakened" or "enlightened", which is really just a more subtle way of entrenching themselves in the Little Me. The moment you feel that you are ready to become a teacher of enlightenment, your journey has taken you in the direction of the Little Me, and it is time to continue on your quest and begin seeking out more clues. These realization clues are here solely to shatter aspects of your Little Me mind so that you can continue into the participatory mindset and begin to see who you really are.

Remember that in general, clues serve two functions. Either they unravel how "real" the world seems and reveal that it's really a game, or they confront us with different aspects of the Little Me, which we can then examine and dismantle, leading us closer to experiencing our true nature. But no clues are designed to be in-your-face obvious. They are designed to be cleverly balanced between urging us to notice what they reveal while also urging our Little Me to label them as random coincidences.

A quick note about psychedelics. Our forest monks at ReWild University almost universally had used psychedelics at some point in their lives, and saw those substances as a "gateway" that launched them on their spiritual journey. At the same time, after a couple of months in the woods and the mental transformations that nature fosters, they reported that the past psychedelic experiences interfered with deeper realizations. If you choose to use psychedelics, remember to use your wisdom. They can spur you forward on your journey and even create powerful insights, but they can also get you tangled in thinking that an "external" is required to allow you to discover Satori's secrets. Like video games, movies, relationships, or anything else in Satori, they can either act as a pitfall or as a clue. Simply note that psychedelics can be a bit trickier than other things, as the experiences they create can mimic realization clues. Remember that regardless of any tools you use, the deepest transformations happen without needing any tools beyond what you have in your own mind.

Morgan Speaks – *Before I began gameplay, I was told that the clues would be tough. They are woven into the game in such a way that the programming of our minds automatically dismisses them or is led away from them. But I was also told that as we start to notice clues, a momentum develops. Clues breed more clues. So look for them, and pay attention to them. They're actually the only really important part of the game. Everything else is just fluff. The more you develop your virtues and attributes, and the deeper you can connect with people and the world, the more clues you'll receive.*

chapter seventeen
EXPERIENCES IN SATORI

Like other RPGs, gameplay in Satori consists of NPCs, but also of situations. These situations or experiences are like "scenes" in a movie, and like a well-crafted movie, every situation is there for a reason. The real magic of these experiences is in the details.

Imagine a team of game designers who have crafted a new open-world game. As they sit down to do a walkthrough of the environment, they will admire the work they've put into things. Grand vistas are beautiful, but the designers will be just as excited about the glint of light off a window, or the way that a shadow responds to a torch's light.

To players, these details often blend into the gameplay. They're not important to the overall story, and the players are not overly conscious of how the details make their gameplay more immersive.

In Satori, we eventually move from being NPCs to being player characters to realizing that we are the creators of the game (remember the three levels of games-within-games that we talked about in Chapter Fifteen?). The more we get into the game-designer mindset, the closer we get to solving Satori. One of the most powerful ways we can get into the game-designer mindset is to start paying attention to the details.

Remember our attributes, virtues, awareness, and wisdom? This is where awareness comes in. Awareness is our ability to go into game-designer mode and notice the details. The more we pay attention to the details, the more awareness we'll cultivate, and the more awareness we cultivate, the more details we'll perceive.

This is one of the trickiest challenges in Satori gameplay. Imagine that a friend comes up to you and starts yelling at you. The Little Me mind, lacking awareness and missing details, sees only the surface of the experience, which is almost always designed as a distraction. Stuck in Little Me, we'll feel offended, feel our pulse increase, and start yelling back. In this way, the experience successfully distracts us and lures us deeper into the Little Me and the non-participatory mindset. We act as NPCs, reacting very predictably.

Now let's encounter that situation again, using awareness and noticing details. Our friend comes up and starts yelling at us. We don't give much attention to the surface experience (the yelling), but instead focus on the details. We notice that our friend has circles under her eyes, and that she has a dark stain on her shirt. Behind her, we see coffee spilled on the table. We now see that our friend didn't get good sleep last night, and just spilled coffee on herself. We may even notice, deep in her expression, the pain she is feeling as she uses us as a punching bag (something she doesn't really want to do). In this experience, we validate her feelings and tell her we understand why she's so angry with us. We ask for forgiveness and offer a hug. Suddenly she breaks down into tears, apologizes, and tells you what is *really* wrong, which has nothing to do with you at all. She just had a lot of pent-up feelings and when the coffee spilled, she lost it and lashed out at the closest person, which was you.

Sometimes your awareness of the details won't transform a situation so dramatically. It might just be that you notice the reflection of a tree in a river, and find yourself soaking into the experience in a way that you weren't a moment before. This is called immersion.

Immersion – *The process of "going deep" into an experience in Satori using awareness. The more we enter immersion, the more our Little Me momentarily dissolves within the given experience, and the more we enter the participatory mindset.*

One way to think of this is to imagine that DM is experiencing Satori through your senses. The more interesting your perceptions are, the more DM will become invested in your gameplay experience. Remember, DM comes from a game designer perspective. A roller coaster ride is interesting, but no more interesting than if you are watching sunlight glint on a spider's web. But there is one clear preference DM has, and that is that our mind-chatter is not very interesting.

In fact, our mind-chatter is the thing that most removes us from immersion. If we are dwelling endlessly on mentally rehearsing the same imaginary conversations with the same people, worrying endlessly about imaginary scenarios, or trying to navigate life by imagining all the things that could go wrong, then DM's experience of "seeing through our senses" isn't going to be very interesting. It's a bit like sitting in front of a TV and watching the same blurry scenes from the same dull soap operas playing over and over. Confronted with that sort of experience through our senses, DM isn't going to pay a lot of attention to making our gameplay more interesting. That's why people who are stuck in those mind-chatter cycles often find their lives repeating the same patterns over and over.

This can be better understood if you imagine that you yourself have designed a huge, open-world game. In this game, you have the ability to watch the actions of any of the players, and even to experience what they are experiencing. You can essentially "go inside" of any character and experience the world through their actions and perceptions. You might enter into an elven character, but the player of the character is so afraid of their character dying that they just stay in a small glen and don't do much of anything except look through their inventory over and over again. Then you switch to someone's half-orc character who is exploring a swamp looking for rare magical reagents. This one is much more interesting, especially as the character is really getting into their world and taking the time to turn over logs, taste berries, and fully immerse themselves in all the details you've created for them.

It's a bit different with DM, because DM can simultaneously be in ALL the characters in the game, and never leaves any of the characters completely. What that means is that if you've been making your gameplay rather uninteresting by just walking in mental circles, you can instantly regain DM's attention the moment you come back into awareness. In fact, as soon as you even begin to make a small effort, DM will focus on your gameplay and immediately begin to make things more interesting. Of course, this is a double-edged sword. On one hand, this means that you'll begin to get more challenges coming your way, but we've already discussed that aspect of the game in Chapter Eleven. On the other hand, after you make your way through enough challenges, DM will start to pull the focus away from challenges and instead start to just enjoy how immersed you are in your everyday experience. Once you can truly enjoy each sip of your hot chocolate, relish the experience of doing dishes, or hear the magic of DM's creation in the barking of a dog, then challenges and problems aren't as necessary, and your gameplay (your "life") starts to become immensely more enjoyable. Because you now thrill in the details, DM will bring all sorts of amazing details into your world, really showing you the very best of DM's game design wizardry. This is when, as we spoke of in Chapter Ten, the Satori gameplay becomes progressively more vibrant and amazing.

To make things even better, DM will also add in more and more clues. The journey toward solving Satori can take on a momentum where everything begins to unfold amazingly. That is, if we can avoid the major pitfalls and traps along the way.

DM Speaks – *Relish the details I have created for you. Every moment of your life is drenched in a thousand details, each of which can fill you with wonder. Beware the habits of mind that will dull your perceptions. Dulled down, your mind will wade through life as if it is thick mud, concentrating only on the effort. Pull your mind from the effort and attend to the details, for I will give you more of whatever you bring your awareness to, or rather, your awareness determines the content of your game. The only true power you have in the game is where you turn the gaze of your mind.*

---

chapter eighteen
TRAPS AND PITFALLS

Remember how psychedelics can act as clever distractions, meant to mimic realization clues? Well, Satori is *filled* with traps and pitfalls of all kinds, and it takes a truly savvy player to avoid them, or get loose once entangled. In this chapter we'll learn about many of the traps waiting for us so that we can navigate Satori more effectively.

A vital thing to remember is that only by strengthening our attributes and virtues and awareness will we develop wisdom, the culmination of all of the attributes. And wisdom is the only thing that will allow us to successfully navigate Satori's traps.

Before we begin, know that unless you develop wisdom to a high degree and with extreme rapidity, you *will* fall prey to traps. Probably many of them. Some may take years to get untangled from. But the traps aren't one-sided. Even when we fall prey to one, it will give us the opportunity to learn, to grow our attributes, and to develop more wisdom. So don't get discouraged. Traps are just part of Satori. Without these challenges, there would be no game to play, and no reason for Satori to exist. So celebrate that traps exist, even as you build your wisdom and become master over them.

Traps are synonymous with distractions, which we've been talking about throughout the book. But now we'll learn about the different types we'll encounter, and as G.I. Joe was fond of telling us, knowing is half the battle.

Remember, our goal in Satori is simple. All we have to do is to break free of the Little Me and remember who we really are. We're playing a character that feels very real to us, and our character is pre-programmed to be prone to distraction. Extremely prone. All we need to do to solve Satori is to learn to turn our minds away from the distractions and/or to make distractions more participatory (which we'll get to in the next chapter). Then we'll begin to see through the matrix, to get clues, and those will lead us forward toward solving the game.

These traps or distractions come in twelve major classes. In this chapter we'll identify them so that you can avoid them if you so desire, while in the next chapter we'll talk about a more advanced and dangerous way to deal with traps, which is to make them more participatory.

Media – This is the most blatant and in-your-face form of distraction that Satori provides. It consists of television shows, news programs, videos, the internet, social media, and all the other tech-based entertainments and social connections that we're offered.

These can steal countless hours from our lives that we could otherwise use in building our attributes or seeking clues, and that's basically what they are designed for. You'll see players in the end-years of their game, stuck in elderly bodies, using their last years watching TV all day long. Others of us will give enormous amounts of time to social media or surfing the internet. Some media can be positive in the sense that it can add knowledge, but even most "educational" offerings are designed as entertainment or are trying to convince you to hold someone else's idea of reality. Most of the media will actively entrench us in the Little Me by leading us into fear and anxiety. Remember that almost all media is designed specifically to continue to program your mind into Little Me thinking, filling us with desires and fears that guide us steadily away from solving Satori.

This media is highly addictive, but it's a visible addiction. You have to be watching a screen or listening to music or otherwise be "plugged in" to feed the addiction. Because it's so visible, it's easier to moderate once we develop some focus and use that to build our attribute of discipline. But until we develop that discipline, media will devour our allotted time in Satori in huge gulps, always decreasing our chances of ultimately solving the game.

To reduce the power of media, we simply need to reduce our consumption of it, change the kind that we consume, or consume it with a participatory mindset. When we take control of our media consumption, we'll shift from being mostly hypnotized to cultivating awareness.

Consumerism – Consumerism is the promise that through buying things, we will make our lives better. But there is a more subtle aspect to consumerism that makes it an even more powerful distraction. We've been pre-programmed to identify ourselves with our possessions. If we own an expensive car, or the latest gaming system, or a trophy house (or trophy spouse, which we often think of as something we own), we add those things onto our Little Me. We imagine ourselves "bigger" with each new thing we own. Our things don't even have to be expensive. We might wear ragged jeans and identify ourselves with those, or drive a beater or electric car or moped, and identify ourselves with that. It's not that we can't use objects to help define our player character – the only question is whether we are doing it consciously or allowing the forces of consumerism to decide it for us.

Consumerism is tied in with media because media includes ads that reinforce the programming that tells us that we're essentially empty and identity-less unless we own the right things.

Like media, consumerism is highly addictive, but also fairly tangible. We can't feed the addiction unless we buy things. Unfortunately, it's difficult to live in Satori without buying things, and many of the things, including food and drinks, can straddle the line between being necessities and being trophies we identify ourselves with. Think of a typical energy drink, with a sex-and-action filled ad that suggests you'll be super bad-ass if you drink it. Ignore the fact that what it *really* does is erode your fitness, drive you closer to diabetes, and throw off your metabolism so that you will eventually pack on more and more fat and look less and less like the people who supposedly drink these things. It's a well-crafted distraction that exploits our weak attributes and virtues and makes us a slave to the ad and the drink, which is itself addictive. Strong attributes and virtues? You'll just laugh at those ads, seeing right through them. Weak attributes and virtues? You'll buy the drink, and the message of the ad will give you a little burst of good feelings as you drink it, even though you'll soon "crash" back into your usual mindset, a little weaker than before you drank it.

This constant purchasing of things distracts us in two ways. First, we have to spend money on things, and money requires either work or money management, even if you are getting passive income. The work or the management both eat up time, of which we have a limited amount in Satori. Secondly, the maintenance of the things we buy requires additional time, money, and energy. A car requires car washes, trips to the repair shop, gas or electricity, and many other types of upkeep. In the end, each thing we own will in turn own us, taking up time and energy that could be used in solving the game, and instead requiring us to spend a lot of our gameplay in managing our inventory of items.

We can better understand consumerism by understanding the concept of "manufactured needs". Tyler Durden sums it up when he's talking to the narrator of *Fight Club.* We're not concerned with anything "real" in life, but rather with needs that have been manufactured for us by people who want our money.

To reduce the power of consumerism, we bring awareness to what we purchase. We ask if something will truly add to our lives, or if the purchase will just cause us to further identify with the Little Me, distracting us from actual gameplay. Note that ads are powerful programming, and few of us have the discipline to resist them. If we turn them off or skip them, that simple action will give us much more power over what we buy.

Games-Within-the-Game – The "games-within-the-game" are our beloved RPGs and video games, *Dungeons and Dragons* and *Call of Cthulu* and any other games that sweep us into becoming another character other than our Little Me. We know that these games hold an important key to Satori, as they give us a direct example of the self-acting-as-player-character dynamic that Satori is built on. Yet we all know that our games can become powerful distractions, sometimes even driving us into addiction. In fact,"games-within-the-game" are often *designed* to be addictive precisely because they hold such powerful clues for us. If we aren't guided by wisdom, and don't have willpower and discipline, the games will be no better than any other media – we'll find ourselves in slave-like obedience to their call, and spend enormous amounts of time playing the same scenes over and over again, trying to accomplish some goal within the game. At some point, however, we'll see that this is a mirror of how we're living in Satori, also trying to accomplish meaningless goals at the cost of actual advancement in the game. Ideally, we'll then stop, shift how we are playing the "game-within-the-game", and integrate the lesson so that we also play Satori differently.

Realize that "games-within-the-game" hold incredible clues. Just be wary of their power to get us "lost" just as Satori gets us lost. Use them with wisdom.

Social Status – Our Little Me has an intense desire to be liked, respected, admired, loved. It will use all sorts of strategies to try to meet that end. Like we saw when we discussed consumerism, it will buy things and identify itself with those things. It will also strive to become "liked" through social media, through leaving comments on forums (including nasty ones, which is the Little Me trying to puff itself up in a very cowardly way, since it doesn't actually have to confront anyone), and through posting self-flattering things on various sites. Little Me can puff itself up through getting educational degrees, a good career, or becoming famous. In its personal relationships, it will try to display certain traits or perform certain actions in order to gain the reactions it craves from other people.

Our Little Me feels very tiny and fragile and afraid, and its main motivation is to puff itself up. But if instead our motivation is to build our attributes and virtues in order to work toward solving Satori, we'll go down a very different road than if we are motivated by getting others to like our Little Me.

World Events – This is tied in with media. As we intake news of wars, terrorist attacks, school shootings, and natural disasters, we can start to carry these "world burdens" with us on a constant basis. If we use personal energy in worrying about, being angry about, or being fearful of things that we're not actively working to fix, we are wasting energy that could otherwise be used in more positive pursuits. We aren't asked to completely ignore world events, but rather to choose how we will participate in things we can fix, and choose not to flood our consciousness with things we can't.

Relationships – Whether we are talking about marriages, friendships, work relationships, or any other type of human connection, relationships basically come in two types. In the first, people are involved in a give-and-take, debt-based relationship where they tend to hold each other back from things. In the other (much more rare), people lift each other up and help each other on their respective journeys. Basically, our relationships can be our greatest source of support, inspiration, and growth, or they can be the biggest life-draining suck in our whole gameplay experience. It's vital that we cultivate the former. The key to this is the virtue of love. If we come to understand this virtue and make it the guiding force in all of our relationships, we will avoid the relationships that devour our life-energy with needless drama, and build the relationships that nurture us and strengthen us.

Body Demands – Monks of all traditions have warned us against the appetites of the body, which can devour enormous amounts of life energy. Our desire for sex, addiction to crappy foods, and the laziness that degrades our bodies – these can dominate our lives. In addition, Satori is laid with some formidable traps in the form of various drugs, such as alcohol and nicotine, that drain money, life energy, and time, while also leading us deeply in the opposite direction of solving Satori.

Yet as Satorians, we aren't called to forsake the body, starve ourselves, be chaste, or be Olympic athletes. Instead, we're asked to immerse ourselves in our experiences. If we have sex, to do it because we feel strongly attached and connected with someone, and want to immerse ourselves in the pleasures we can experience together with them. When we eat food, to truly savor it, and to choose foods that foster mental clarity and build the attribute of fitness. This makes the Satorian path different – it's not about denying things, but rather making good choices and truly enjoying the choices we make. Wisdom and discipline will help us to monitor our relationship with our body and its insistent demands. Will we be slaves to its every whim, allowing it to distract us in sexual relationships that never really satisfy, to addict us to foods that drag us down, and to lure us into vices like smoking that chain us to manufactured needs? Or will we hear our bodies calling, make a conscious decision of whether and how to answer, and thus take the helm?

Mind-Chatter – All of that media, drama, temptation, and desire to be liked creates a lot of stuff to think about. And our minds, celebrated in-game as being the pinnacle of evolution but actually consisting mainly of programming meant to lead us astray, are extremely fond of using all of that information to tell endless stories. With Forest Monks at ReWild University, we often call this "storytelling". What it means is that we can spend huge amounts of time and energy talking to ourselves, usually silently, often rehearsing imaginary conversations with bosses, friends, family members, and co-workers. If it's not those conversations, our mind is carrying on a dialog or steeping itself in feelings about future worries, past regrets, wrongs done unto us, and many other forms of mind-chatter. We're programmed so that this storytelling is habitual, which means that our mind-chatter is almost constant. This is one of the most powerful things that keeps us from solving Satori, because it acts as a kind of blurry filter that makes the whole world feel like an old-fashioned TV with static. We simply don't experience much except for our chatter, and DM gets disinterested in the chatter and gives us what we seem to be asking for — just more static to take up our time.

Note that mind-chatter is quite a different thing from conscious, deliberate thought. That kind of thinking is indeed a powerful tool. But mind-chatter leads us into unconsciousness, from which we will judge, get ever-more-tangled in the Little Me, and basically lose ourselves in the game.

Our tool for avoiding mind-chatter is focus. Mind-chatter hijacks our focus and directs it again and again to our internal storytelling. As we learn to point our focus where we want it, we can simply direct it away from mind-chatter and toward something else. The trick is finding something interesting enough to our minds that it will capture our attention. Of course, if we've been developing discipline, we can direct our minds largely where we choose. But until then, we have to cater to our minds' tastes. Ideally we can choose this moment we're experiencing – the sights, sounds, and other sensations that are present in the current scene we're in. Continually shift your focus onto the current scene, and you will build discipline and reduce your mind-chatter, while also being able to recognize when the chatter is happening and shift your focus away from it.

Autopilot – Closely related to mind-chatter is autopilot, a state of being "zoned out" that is familiar to most of us. The typical example is when you're driving, and you suddenly realize you have been driving through stoplights and making turns for the past five minutes, and you've been in zombie mode the whole time, completely unaware of where you were or the passing of time.

This is a handy function of our minds, to be able to

take over when we're on a mental vacation. But it also becomes habitual, and many of us spend a lot of time in autopilot. In fact, for most of us, we'll wake up in the morning, quickly move into mind-chatter, and when our minds become exhausted, we will "rest" in autopilot, then go back into chatter, then back to autopilot . . . you see how it goes.

Our awareness and practice of paying attention to the details is our pathway out of autopilot. It will happen gradually just through building our attributes and virtues, but we can speed our way out of autopilot with any meditation practice. All of them will help us master autopilot and take back our minds.

Inner Negativity – A subtle form of mind-chatter combined with autopilot, inner negativity is easy to fall into. This is the inner critic, who is always telling us we are losers, unworthy, not really, really, really ridiculously good looking, or just plain worthless. It will jump onto almost anything we do and tell us how we've done it wrong. Not satisfied with ourselves, it also judges others, spending a lot of time thinking how other people are idiots, wimps, or jerks. This is the voice of the Little Me, who gets a lot of attention when it is feeling bad about itself. Since your Little Me certainly doesn't want other people to be better than it is, it focuses on other people's Little Mes. It doesn't see DM in other people – it only sees the illusion presented by Satori.

Inner negativity requires mind-chatter to keep reinforcing its message of self-loathing and other-criticizing, and requires autopilot to keep those negative thoughts running in the background. So the good news is that as you take on the challenges of mind-chatter and autopilot, you'll automatically make progress with inner negativity. But you can make additional progress by learning to laugh at yourself, and starting to see DM in everyone you meet (we'll talk about this more in Chapter Twenty-Two).

Pride – As easily as we can fall into inner negativity, we can also fall into pride. The amount of time we spend boasting of our qualities only makes those around us uncomfortable, because others can always sense the deep insecurity inside of prideful people. Often, as someone launches into stories of how great they are, those around them become quiet, mindful of how easily the prideful person will be hurt if anyone calls them out. When we find ourselves bragging, we know we are trying to puff up the Little Me to hide from our own fears. We can make a shift and move forward in the game if we stop and ask why we are feeling this need to build ourselves up in the eyes of others (sound reminiscent of our talk regarding social status?), especially when deep down, we know that we're only exposing how insecure our Little Me really is.

Asking why will bring us back to remembering that the Little Me is not who we really are, and remind us that any action we use to puff it up is only leading us in the wrong direction. The sooner we can give up the desire to impress others, the sooner we will find that energies are freed up to move closer to solving Satori.

Note that pride is not the same as being aware of your inherent value, or of honoring the skills you've developed. The skills you develop are vital tools to solving Satori. Just don't get distracted into being your own cheering squad. Concentrate on how your skills apply to the game.

Gaze-Turning – The good news about gaze-turning is that it is a trap in the game that is only triggered once you are pretty far along the route toward solving Satori. Once you are consistently seeing clues, gaze-turning is turned on in your game. It functions by waiting until you are experiencing a realization clue, when you really feel you're on the verge of "getting" something. You might be talking with someone about it, or just feeling it yourself, and then your phone will ring, or someone will walk into the room, or you'll drop something. The distraction can come in a thousand forms, but it is designed to turn your gaze away from the realization and make you pay attention to some other element of the game. It will probably begin to happen fairly consistently, and you'll find that many potential realization clues are lost by gaze-turning.

While gaze-turning is certainly distracting, it's also a last-ditch trap that is put in place to give some final challenges before you really start to figure out Satori. The trap will turn off as soon as you begin to resist the gaze-turning and stay on track.

Here's a concrete example. You just were hit with a powerful realization of who DM really is. A fellow Satorian is there, and you feel that if you can explain it to her, it will benefit you both. You start trying to explain your realization, and suddenly the neighbor's dog pushes through the front door and jumps onto your couch. Choice A is to yell at the dog and try to shoo it out, at which point the neighbor comes over and apologizes and gets you to engage in a five-minute conversation. By the time you close the door and turn to your friend, the realization has faded. Choice B is to laugh a little since you recognize gaze-turning for what it is, sit down next to the dog on your couch, and pet him while you explain to your friend how DM is really this dog.

Consistently choose not to engage with gaze-turning on its terms, but rather on yours, and soon it will turn off and you'll be free of its powers.

We've mentioned wisdom a number of times in this chapter. But what is this wisdom? It is the blossoming of knowledge, taking information such as what you found in this chapter and then integrating it so that you begin to see past the distractions and behold the clues (and ultimately the final truth that results in solving Satori) that have long been hiding in plain sight. It emerges naturally as you cultivate the other virtues, and serves to always guide you on the right path.

Morgan Speaks – *Is Satori for you or against you? At some point you might find yourself asking that question. Remember, like in any game, it's both. The game is designed to give you a real chance of solving it. But it wouldn't be a game if it wasn't challenging. And Satori is hyper-challenging, while still being balanced. Don't give up! I'm depending on you!*

---

chapter nineteen

MAKING DISTRACTIONS MORE PARTICIPATORY

In the not-too-distant future, Prakriti Coding will be discovered. Unlike most current coding, in which every detail must be made up of 1's and 0's, Prakriti Coding is a completely different paradigm. Here, one is not typing code into a computer, but "coding" tiny biological systems. In Prakriti Coding, a small, unique "Core" is created, and from that Core every detail and element of a game emerges. What this means is that every detail of a game coded in Prakriti leads back to the Core. Every detail IS the Core. And the Core is every detail, much like a holograph in which every detail contains the entire picture.

For us, this means that you can solve Satori through any detail or element of the game. "To see a world in a grain of sand." (Remember Blake?) This means that even all of the traps and pitfalls can lead us straight to solving Satori, IF we can make them participatory and follow them to the Core. In effect, this allows us to self-generate clues. It's an artform, and as we mentioned in the last chapter, it is both difficult and dangerous. But if you want to take on the challenge, this chapter will tell you how.

Wait? Dangerous? What I mean is that if we choose this route, we give ourselves a powerful opportunity to erode the Little Me at the same time that we give the Little Me many chances (with each distraction we try to transform) to reinvent itself in new and more subtle ways. If we don't have immense wisdom, all we'll succeed in doing is creating an ever-more-subtle and ever-more-entrenched Little Me who pretends to have solved Satori. But in truth, we will only have succeeded in getting ourselves more lost in the game.

Despite this danger, most of us will decide to attempt to transform at least some of the distractions in our game. We want certain things in our gameplay, and are willing to take the time, energy, and risk necessary to have those things. For instance, early in my life I decided I wanted to spend my whole gameplay with my wife, Rebecca. We spent many years in self-created drama, using up immense amounts of energy in the process. Yet at the same time, both of us seemed to know that we could help each other in our respective journeys, and we opted to stick things out. Twenty years later, we decided to have children, another thing that would take immense amounts of life energy. But because we saw all of our own dramas and all the challenges of parenting as part of our journey in Satori, we were slowly able to transform these elements so that they became powerful tools for growth. Now, we have a relationship where we don't generate drama, and are able to help each other forward in the game by leaps and bounds. We wanted each other in our games, and were willing to take the time to transform a normal (dramatic) relationship into becoming the best possible companions for each other in our journey, able to support and challenge each other at the same time.

Now that you know about distractions, you might decide that some, like alcohol or an abusive relationship, can be removed from your life. But you might decide that others, like gaming or your favorite cupcakes, can stay. It only remains to transform the distractions we choose to keep. We must further understand where we get "lost" in Satori and where we can progress in positive ways. And we use the cupcake to call us to awareness, to invite DM to enjoy the cupcake through our senses, and thereby to encourage DM to enrich our gameplay experience. We must just take care to be aware of when we eat the cupcake mindlessly, out of habit and body demands that we are helpless to resist. To transform a distraction, we must be fully conscious of the activity we're engaging in.

An example. You're about to hit the power button

on your gaming console, or role a die during a game of D&D. As you reach out to touch the plastic, you can do it mindlessly, just like any other time you've ever done it. Or, you can immerse yourself in the experience. Feel, mentally, what the moment before pressing the button or picking up the die feels like. Pause when your skin touches the plastic, and experience the tactile sensation. Feel the smoothness, the temperature. And as you push the button or roll the die, feel the tactile sensations, notice what you see and hear, and again tune in to the mental sensations generated by the action. Is there a relief of some inner tension, feelings of excitement or nervousness or guilt, or a feeling of expectation?

This is an everyday, "normal" experience, but like every detail in Satori, it holds enormous clues. It's just that usually, those clues pass us by because our focus isn't directing our awareness in a positive way.

Seen like this, we discover that the entire world of Satori is one big distraction. After all, it is designed to create the perfect hiding place where we can elude ourselves through a thousand means. This is the simple pattern that is found throughout Satori – look only on the surface, and we will further entangle ourselves in belief systems, programming, and lifeways that lead us further into delusion. But if we look past the superficial and see deep into any detail of Satori, we will be led to wisdom. Every detail leads to the Core, to DM. And DM is found in every detail. You are one of those details. YOU (your Little Me) are one of the distractions, ready to be transformed.

Remember that it's all about things becoming participatory. Our minds will be turned this way and that, called and beckoned by a thousand distractions. To solve Satori, we must no longer be controlled by these distractions, but must instead transform them, and see what is waiting when we finally see through the matrix.

Cowan Faol Speaks – *I am beloved by most people in my world, but some despise me. And one common critique among those folks is that I just use my magic for creating pleasures for myself. In some ways, that's a fair criticism. For instance, I love to conjure myself and my friends fabulous food – because it emerges from magic, no plants or animals need to die, and I can make things that are ridiculously delicious. Omelets with bacon inside that stays perfectly melt-in-your mouth crispy. Ice cream that remains at that perfect cold-but-melty state for as long as it takes you to eat it. Layered drinks where the layers never mix. And much of my food is individually made to go straight to your "pleasure centers", to remind you of your grandmother's cooking, or otherwise invoke emotions or memories that enhance the flavors. Why do I use my magic for such "petty" things? Because to DM, the everyday moments of life are as important as anything else. Our Little Me can enjoy something, and DM gets to enjoy that thing through us. The essential part to remember is that we can either get lost in an experience or get immersed in an experience. This might seem like the same thing, but it's not. Lost, we eat the food mindlessly, gobbling down a cake or imbibing a drink without actually tasting it. Immersed, we savor it as if it's the last thing we'll eat or drink in our entire lives. When I make my food so delicious, it's to sweep my friends into being totally present – a slice of Cowan-cake is so mind-blowingly delicious that you have little choice but to be totally immersed in every single bite. In this way, I give my friends entrance into their DM nature just by serving them a bowl of ice cream. You may not be getting Cowan-food anytime soon (though we will perhaps meet at some point and I won't forget to serve you your favorite treat), but you can still choose to immerse yourself in the next experience you encounter. It might be eating a sandwich, riding a horse, making love, or plugging in a game console. Whatever you do, immerse yourself in it, and you'll begin to enter into another world – a world that's been waiting for you right in plain sight.*

chapter twenty

THE INNER WORKINGS OF SATORI

By now we understand the basics of how Satori works, and have at least an inkling of what is waiting for us if we start to play effectively instead of just continuing to get lost in Satori's distractions. Let's look deeper into the game, which will help us in gameplay, and even allow us to start modding the game a little bit.

In Satori, we've been thrust into an ultra-realistic open world RPG where we chose to become "lost" in a character. At first, that character basically functions as an NPC, lost in autopilot, mind-chatter, and distractions. We *believe* we are in control, but we're only in the first level of gameplay, where the goal is to realize that we're not in control, and to begin to transform our relationship with the game elements so that we begin to take the helm. The evolution here is something like going from playing Pac-

Man, where there are some minor choices but our actions are largely dictated by the environment, to going to an open world RPG, where you can choose from almost innumerable options.

You can probably see how Satori works in the same way. Most people feel like their life is laid out before them with few choices. Depending on your parenting, there can be enormous pressure to finish high school and join the military, or go to tech school, or go to college, or go to graduate school. Debt steps in and locks us down into jobs. We get married on impulse and get tangled in bad relationships. This is the Pac-Man version of the game, which is where most people are stuck, making choices based on external pressures rather than what we know will be good for us.

Intertwined in the events we experience in this Pac-Man level are many hints of how we can break free. We hear about Daniel Suelo and other people living without money, even as we drive to work *again* because there are endless bills to pay. Fear convinces us that maybe Daniel can go moneyless, but we never could. Fear convinces us that someone else can sail around the world, but we can't. Someone else can open a restaurant, become a game designer, start their own line of gourmet ice cream, become a world adventurer, or write a book. But because of our allegiance to fear, we can't.

Fear – *A desire for "security" that blocks us from paying attention to any clues. This fear lures us into doing the same thing for years or decades, even if it is quite uncomfortable. Some examples would be staying in a bad relationship (it would be too messy to try to break up), continuing to go to a job we hate (it gets good benefits), or getting lost in negative habits (they are strangely comforting).*

Thus, to break past level one, we need to shake free of fear and see that we are in an open world game. The limits placed upon us are mostly self-imposed. The game world is filled with possibilities, and as we develop our attributes and virtues, more possibilities open up to us. If we can avoid prison, soul-sucking jobs, drug addictions, bad relationships, negative self-talk/low self-esteem, and other ways in which the level-one game tries to pin us down, we're on our way toward level two. Still, fear will stand in our way. One way to overcome fear is to see the futility of security.

To recognize this, we have only to look around us. My father once told me a story of a fellow student in medical school who was going to be a brain surgeon. He worked and toiled endlessly, stressing about tests, studying constantly, and devoting his life to getting his degree, his eyes fixed on becoming a surgeon and living the life of esteem and money that the career would bring him. He graduated with flying colors, and a week later was killed in a car accident.

It's fine to work on a degree, but if we want to get anywhere in the game, it's essential that as we work toward our degree, we are also working on our attributes and virtues, and immersing ourselves in the present moment instead of just being fixated on a distant goal. The end of our time in Satori can come at any moment, so how we spend our time is vital. And it's not just "death" that can remove our security. Our finances can disappear with the loss of a job or a shift in the stock market, or our health can evaporate in an unexpected diagnosis. The idea is not to start playing the game (and really LIVING) at some time in the future when we have everything lined up "just right", but to start playing and living right NOW.

Remember, no situation in Satori is a game-ender in and of itself. If you're in prison, you can still play. If you're going into the military or tech school, you can still play. Even if you are stuck in drug addiction, you can still play. But in order to play effectively, we need to break free of these things ruling our lives. They can be things we are *doing*, but they are not who we *are*.

As we free ourselves of being pinned down by these things and let go of security, we enter level two play. This is what most of this book is about, since you've probably already recognized the futility of clinging to fantasies of security and are ready to journey onward. We've discussed many of the traps we'll encounter, but as we look even deeper into Satori, we can notice a few other ways that the game tries to keep us lost in illusion.

A huge one is judgment in all its forms. I know we've already talked about this, but I want to re-emphasize it because it is so important. We must beware emotions like the desire for revenge or "justice". These are glorified in movies and games, yet the moment we exact revenge is the moment we strengthen our Little Me, who for a moment feels like it really can have power over the world. But the Little Me is truly powerless, just a frightened little ghost who clings to anything that will make it feel more real.

When we judge others as less advanced/intelligent/wise than ourselves, we make the same mistake. We might look at ourselves and feel that we've entered level two gameplay, and then it's easy to look at others and think how those poor lost souls are still stuck in level one, brainless NPCs without a clue. Again, this is the Little Me trying to puff itself up. Yes, we can reach out and help others (which we'll learn more about soon), but the moment we do that from a place of superiority is the moment that we show ourselves still lost in the Little Me.

In level two, Satori will give us all sorts of problems. These are not there to be solved in the orthodox sense, but rather to teach us something. Again, our virtues are our guides here. Imagine that we don't have enough money to pay our bills, and we're going to lose our house. We know we can sell those prescription opiate pills that have been in our medicine cabinet and make a lot of money. We realize we'll just be feeding someone's addiction, that we're weakening our virtues, but we do it anyway. When we do, Satori sees that you are giving power to the idea of lacking money, and are effectively getting yourself lost in trying to solve the problem of paying the bills. The game mechanics kick in to give you this same problem again, since it obviously was effective in getting you more lost. In this way, you'll continue in the same cycle month after month, unwittingly invoking Satori's game mechanics to keep you pushed back toward level one. It's not the world doing this to us – it is our own decisions that keep invoking the same cycles, much like in a video game where we keep taking the left-hand passage again and again and keep getting killed by the dragon, all the while ignoring that we could just as easily try the right-hand passage.

You can probably hear your Little Me screaming out its warnings. "Don't listen! If you don't sell the oxycodone, you'll lose the house!" Well, maybe you will. And that will lead to a new chapter in your adventure. Or maybe you'll call the bank and they'll help you out a little bit. Or maybe you'll inherit some money. Or maybe you'll be offered a much better-paying job that you actually enjoy. One thing is for sure. Choose the wrong passage, and you'll just keep in the cycle. Cultivate your virtues and be guided by them, and opportunities will open up. Sometimes they'll do it in frightening ways (like losing the house), but when you look back after some time has passed, it will be clear why Satori led you down the path it did. Because like any good game, it wants to give you challenges, but also wants to give you a fighting chance to solve the game.

Note that it's not just doing something "immoral", like selling drugs, that keeps us locked into cycles of getting lost. It might be things that others consider very sensible, like staying in a well-paying job even though it's sucking out your soul. In general, in level two, the "right" decisions are not the easy ones or the ones that others are urging you toward. Ignore that guy that insists all your problems can be solved if you open a meth lab, or the well-meaning friend who tells you to go and apply for the job that you know you'll hate. Remember that the way forward might look upside-down to most people, especially those living by fear (which includes both the meth-lab guy and the friend). There will be many influences that try to convince you toward the wrong path. Whether they are religions, financial schemes, life philosophies, or any other thing the game offers up, notice if it is based in fear. Only take advice if it challenges your fear and points you toward those special things that dwell at the fringes of your courage – the things that you know will take you on a true adventure and fill your heart.

Since money is a huge challenge for most of us, here's a final hint to deal with it in the game. Remember that it's not about having "enough" money, because money can rule your life whether you are homeless or you're a billionaire. Instead, it's about not having to worry about money, and you can accomplish that with a billion dollars in the bank, by living money-free, or by anything in between. It's not about how much of the external you have, but rather what is happening inside of you. Consider this carefully, as it applies to much more than money.

Here's another thing to remember. In addition to problems in level two, Satori will give us good things. And these good things, far from being the holy grails we're told they are, are actually just as dangerous (if not more so) than problems. Make a boatload of money, and your life may very well plunge back into level one, with all of your attention going to the new task of managing your funds and purchasing endless distractions. "Good" or "bad", the situations brought into our game by Satori in level two are all there for the same purpose – to push us back toward level one (if we're not cultivating our attributes and virtues) while simultaneously giving us hidden gateways into level three (if we are cultivating those attributes and virtues).

A final spoiler. Surrender is key. When we let go into

the game (which fear will resist with all its strength), the game will switch up and start to push us forward into level three play. This is where the traps and "external" challenges of Satori fall away, as they are no longer challenging for us (remember that Satori will only keep a challenge in our game so long as it challenges us). In level three, we start to see who we are, and spend a lot of time getting realization clues and beginning to choose a route into becoming DM. And that, my friends, we will talk about more in Chapter Twenty-Two.

To sum up, remember that in level one, we're basically lost, and our job is to shake free of the illusion that is pinning us down. In level two, Satori throws the hordes at us, giving us challenge after challenge, problem after problem. Here, our job isn't to solve these problems in the "real world", but to start to undo the game's need to keep throwing these problems at us. It's fine to solve problems or work through them, but always learn from each one and choose pathways out that don't ask the game to give you the problems again and again (sometimes in the same forms, sometimes in slightly different forms). In level two, our attributes and virtues will be the tools that will move us forward through the hordes. We must resist the temptations of fear and begin to immerse ourselves in our gameplay. Then, level three will begin to unfold in front of us.

Morgan Speaks – *You know that pesky question of free will? Well, do we have it or not? The answer in Satori, of course, is both. When we start the game, we have very few choices, and the main trick is that the game fools us into thinking our "choices" are ours while we're actually on autopilot. So in level one, we have to snap out of this illusion and realize that we're basically puppets. The moment we do that is the moment we start to gain some freedom of thought and action. In level two we start to gain more and more free will, and also more and more power over the game world – not by the old means of trying to manipulate things with our words or physical actions, but by something more like magic – a sort of paradoxical release into the game which allows us to manifest things along the way. But while this great stuff is happening in level two, Satori is also actively throwing us all kinds of challenges that try to convince us that we're powerless and send us back to level one. In level three, things get super magical. So it's basically a spectrum where on one side we're powerless automatons, and on the other side we're approaching our DM nature, which can manifest worlds without even trying. Between the two is all of us – me, and you, and Cowan, and Kenton – and hopefully we all keep moving in the direction of our DM nature instead of plummeting backward to level one.*

chapter twenty-one

WHAT IS THE LITTLE ME?

You've heard over and over again that the "me" we think of as ourselves is really a character we're playing, and that this character is our Little Me. This Little Me is a construct, much like a character we roll up in AD&D, with a name, attributes, skills, and a personality. But unlike in AD&D, we don't remember rolling up our character. We did indeed create it, and we created the perfect character to give us that sweet-spot balance between making the game ultra-challenging and also making it possible to solve. But when we launched our game, the technology of Satori erased our memory of who we really are (well, actually it just tucked it away someplace safe), created an entire memory past for our character, and pre-programmed our new minds with all sorts of desires, fears, ideas, and beliefs that point us in the wrong direction of solving the game.

This character, this Little Me, is utterly convincing. It was a simple but smart move to stock the game with innumerable artifacts from your past – photos and old teddy bears, baby footprints and letters from old crushes. Archived web pages, YouTube videos of ads you remember from childhood, funny stories your friends tell about you. And of course endless memories. All of these draw us into the illusion that there is a past, and that past helps us to sculpt the Little Me in our imagination. It's a feeling, too. We're given the Little Me sensation, as if we are a tiny driver up in our skulls, looking out through our eyes. And most of us are given a world-view that continues to support the Little Me fantasy – a world-view that tells us we are one little bag of flesh in a huge, vast, and mostly hostile universe (except the area immediately surrounding us, which we do our best to keep Mostly Harmless).

The Little Me is this frightened little bag, looking out at the endless stars and galaxies, knowing that it is utterly insignificant, and then because of that fear, it starts making as much noise and fuss as it can in order to make itself seem important.

From everything we've heard so far, we can think that the goal of the game is to destroy the Little Me. But that's not true at all. Instead, we're called to recognize that the Little Me is a character, and then everything changes.

It's as if you were playing an RPG, and you forgot you were playing and started to think the RPG world was real. Even if you had been a fearless adventurer, you'd suddenly be fearful for your life. You might very well decide it's time to stop adventuring and do something safer, like open a cupcake shop in your home village. You'd become satisfied with running the store day after day, even it is was terrifically boring, because it feels secure. But the moment you remembered that you were just a character, you'd throw off your flour-stained apron and head out adventuring again. Fear would no longer hold you back from what you love.

This is the dynamic of the Little Me at work. The Little Me tries to encase itself in a secure little bubble from which it can criticize and peer out at the world. It won't step out of that bubble, because it fears what is waiting outside. It tries to ignore the fact that it's just as likely to die from a car accident or from eating fast food as it is from going on a hike in the mountains or learning to surf. So it calls wild ideas "stupid" and steers us in the direction of getting more and more lost in Satori. If we dare to step out of the Little Me, forces around us will often swoop in and try to push us back. For instance, family or friends might remind us that our ideas are ridiculous, that we're being too foolish or risky or idealistic.

Now, you might be thinking that you don't really like your character. Maybe it's not very good looking, or not witty, or it needs to use a wheelchair, or it sucks at math. But as you transform the Little Me, you'll find that the wheelchair doesn't always have to be a liability, but can also be a blessing. Or that your failures at math are more than made up for in your ability to draw. You might even find that many of the qualities you wish you had were always there, just hiding behind a lot of fear.

Some people might think that the Little Me needs to die in order to move forward. Again, this isn't true at all (unless we mean a figurative death). Your Little Me has been chosen very carefully by YOU, and it holds everything necessary to enjoy your gameplay experience, and also to solve Satori. Of course, we will all die at some point in this game, and then wake up either immersed in a new game (if we haven't solved Satori) and having to play all over again, or else we solve Satori and wake up as the game-designer, able to enter the game much like Cowan Faol, as player and designer simultaneously. This is becoming DM, the result of solving Satori, and eventually, we'll all get there.

DM Speaks – *The person you think you are is in truth only me, hiding from myself. But this incarnation is not to be discarded, for it is the whole purpose of this game. Without Little Mes who have forgotten who they are, lost in dramas and pains and pleasures, I would not be able to hide from myself. There would be no game, and without the game, DM is only silence. You are the instrument, the violin whose strains weave the world together, give meaning to the stars, creating the rainbows. There is nothing you are not, and nothing that is not you. Your Little Me is the game itself, so do not seek to destroy it, but rather to transform it.*

chapter twenty-two

WHO IS DM?

Remember how we talked about myth? Everything in this book is in the language of myth, but it's especially important to remember in this chapter. All the words here are merely pointers, trying to turn our gaze toward entering level three and then solving Satori.

To really understand this idea of myth, consider the color purple. Now imagine that you have a friend who has been blind from birth. She wants to experience the color purple. You sit down across a table and try to describe it to her. But no matter how well you craft your words or how many years you spend trying to describe it, the best you will do is form an idea in her mind, and it won't equate with purple. Purple isn't something she can experience from your description, because it is a direct experience.

Direct Experience – *When we perceive something with our senses in its pure form, without adding words that skew our perceptions or create an image in our heads.*

You can apply this color example to yourself as well. Many insects and birds can see into the ultraviolet range. They are seeing an array of colors that is as different as yellow is from green. If we could see in this range and beyond, we'd perceive more layers in each rainbow, seeing colors that no human has ever seen. Online, you can find side-by-side photos of birds or flowers, one labeled as "human vision" and one (more colorful) labeled as "bird vision". But don't be fooled. These pictures can give us an imaginary idea of what a bird sees, but they can only substitute colors we can see (or else we wouldn't see them). What a bird actually sees is *totally different colors*. Try to imagine those other colors. What do they look like? We can only form an idea in our heads, but we can't actually experience them.

See how this works? On the one hand we have direct experience, and on the other hand we have our words that try to describe direct experience. But if you think about it, words can never describe direct experience. Words can only act to trade ideas between two minds. Can you describe love to someone who has never felt it, and give them the direct experience of falling in love through your description? Can you give someone the taste of vanilla ice cream with your words, or the sensation of skydiving? We can imagine all of these things, but they aren't the same as direct experience. Even if you take something concrete, like a concrete block, and try to describe it to me, we're just trading an idea from mind to mind. The picture of a concrete block you have in your head will differ to a greater or lesser degree from the picture I have formed in my mind.

This is the nature of words. They can transmit ideas, but never direct experience, and even the ideas transmitted are seldom what we think they are.

This is essential to understand, otherwise we will spend immense amounts of energy mistaking pointers for direct experiences, and our daily experience will be less about what is actually around us, and more about experiencing other people's fantasies in our heads.

With this fresh in our minds, let's look at some myths that will point us in the direction of understanding DM.

DM is the ultimate truth behind Satori. It is the creator of Satori, but also *is* Satori. We could think of DM as the great game designer, who crafted a game so potent that even DM could lose itself in the game. This, after all, is the goal of any movie or game – to immerse us so deeply in the creation that we forget ourselves, and the game or movie starts to seem "real".

Now, how can DM be the creator of Satori and *be* Satori at the same time? This riddle has confused the minds of religious and spiritual folks down through the centuries. Even a monotheistic religion like Christianity insists that God became Jesus, who *is* God and yet is also a separate thing from God. Our rational minds want to insist it has to be one or the other, but there it is in the world's most popular religion – Jesus is both man and God simultaneously.

Hinduism was laying out a similar concept much earlier, with Brahman who is simultaneously all that is, and also completely unknowable. Brahman is the other Hindu gods, is you and me, is the plate of spaghetti you ate for dinner last night, and yet is none of these things.

The Hindus thus are closest to what we mean by DM, because when we say "lost", DM is not just becoming lost in people. DM becomes lost in the form of stones, rainbows, dreams, diamonds, snapping turtles, and multivitamins. *Everything* in the game is DM. And yet to try to define DM, even using the Hindu version, will only lead us to create a picture in our minds, like our blind friend's picture of the color purple, and we'll then miss the real DM that is waiting for us in direct experience.

DM's technology (or spirituality, however you want to see it) is so advanced that DM can be all of these things simultaneously. Our Little Me minds can't comprehend being more than one thing at a time (or maybe two or three if we are exceptionally creative). We can perhaps imagine that DM could jump from being one thing to another to another, but we can't wrap our heads around being every speck of dust, every grain of sand, every elephant and rose and supernova and towel in the universe. All. At. Once.

Still, this is what DM is doing, becoming the open world of Satori in its every detail. We can grasp it a little if we imagine that if we were in DM's perspective, we could become any person or creature or thing, any time in the history or the future of the universe. This is an important point, because it's reassuring to the Little Me to know that if it does indeed solve Satori and become DM, nothing is lost. You can go back to being "you" (the Little Me) any time you want.

Moreover, DM is not limited to the version of Satori that you are experiencing right now. DM is every detail in this Satori, but also in an infinite number of other Satoris. The world of Carador that Rebecca and I "invented" is a Satori that DM can play in. Indeed, DM can play in any of a million, billion Satoris, choosing worlds of magic or darkness, worlds of heavenly bliss, worlds of unbelievable technology or simple living, worlds of alien civilizations, of lost worlds in distant galaxies, worlds of dragon-riders, worlds of robots, worlds beyond our imagination. Every world ever created by humans is another Satori, every world YOU have imagined is a Satori. And as DM, those worlds are your playground, with you as every single character experiencing every single situation.

If our minds prefer science, DM is still waiting for us there. Science is searching for a great "something" that rests at the base of reality. We hope to understand it through a Theory of Everything, and we continue to grow closer to that realization. If and when science finds the TOE, it will have unified a universe that before seemed chopped into parts. Science may find that consciousness is the unification, or it may find that it's all vibrating strings, or discover that there is a core that is paradoxically a singularity while also being all that exists. In any case, the scientific quest for the ultimate nature of reality leads us just as effectively toward discovering DM, for DM is the unknowable source of all that is.

We can begin, then, to see glimpses of DM. DM is not afraid to experience terrible things. Nor is DM averse to experiencing wonderful things. In fact, DM does not even differentiate – experiences are experiences, with pain as worthy an experience as pleasure. DM does not judge. But DM does take a special interest in those places where DM begins to remember, to discover itself. Because in every Satori DM has scattered clues, and when one of DM's guises starts to discover those clues, things become really fun. It's as if you created an open world game and are watching all the NPCs you created, and then all of the sudden one starts talking to you. It becomes "alive", like a doll in a children's tale, and to your surprise it knows who you are and what's going on. Then, that character becomes extra fun to watch and interact with, especially as it begins to understand the inner workings of the game and starts to develop something akin to magic.

DM is the Ultimate that so many are seeking. Scientists seek DM in the Theory of Everything. Christians seek DM in God. Taoists seek DM in the Tao, Hindus in Brahman.

Another way to imagine DM is like the Dungeon Master in D&D, who co-creates the game with the player characters at the table, manifesting the setting, the NPCs, the encounters, the challenges, and the rewards. When Rebecca is the Dungeon Master for me (as Cowan), she is like the Hindu Brahman, incarnating herself as everything and everyone Cowan meets. Nothing and no one in Cowan's world is not Rebecca. She is all-powerful, but has no need to prove or flaunt that power as a human ego would. Her power is used solely to craft an ongoing story for Cowan. Cowan is a character in the story, but he is also me, and he also knows that even though his world seems very real, it is all invoked by DM, by Rebecca. And Cowan, through me, can influence DM to make the world appear more as Cowan would like it, and through his own rendering (which we will explore in Chapter Twenty-Six), plays a co-creationary role with DM/Rebecca.

This is like Morgan, who is playing you. And as you come to realize the true nature of Satori, you see that

Morgan is DM, and through you, Morgan sees that the creators of Satori are DM. And those creators, through the chain of you and Morgan, see that the Ultimate is DM, creating all of this, games-within-games, a beautiful tangle from which a few of us might wake up to realize that there is nothing happening except for DM.

It can help to personify DM. Though DM is beyond words, and can only be pointed to with myth, we can start to tap into a connection with DM by personifying it and trying to approach DM from one angle or another. The rational-minded person might approach DM by exploring Theories of Everything, and in that way come to understand more about DM through that lens. The Christian might approach DM in the guise of God, and in that way develop a closer connection through that lens. Rebecca and I borrowed the Hindu concept of Divine Mother, who is our DM. And the concept we choose will help shape the game play we experience. In the past, when Rebecca and I thought of DM in a more linear, scientific guise, our lives were more random and felt a bit less warm and human. With Divine Mother, our lives manifest loving people, warmth, and kindness. Many Christians we know find their lives alternately filled with blessings and then with tragedy, mimicking the God presented in the Bible who has two very different faces depending on which part of the Bible you are reading.

Rebecca and I use this concept of Divine Mother to

give us something our Little Me minds can attach to, to start building a relationship with DM. For DM is both us and not-us, is truly Divine Mother and is truly not, and until we find our own DM nature, there are many advantages to interacting with DM as another being or concept. We pray to Divine Mother, and bring her into our daily life by inviting her to taste food through our mouths, enjoy the forest through our eyes when we go for a walk, and feel the pain/pleasure of a good run or workout. This draws us into the present moment, making our characters' experiences more interesting to DM. We also look around and consciously see Divine Mother in the autumn leaves along the trail, in the face of the stranger we meet, and the barking of the neighbor's dog. In this way we break down our conception of separateness and reinforce the participatory mindset. And we remind ourselves that we are Divine Mother, playing our characters, which helps us to release our attachment to Little Me. All the while, Divine Mother's all-loving nature fills us constantly with happiness, joy, and a sense of security that doesn't depend on money, people, or other "externals". This keeps us in a positive mindset that isn't interested in drama, inner negativity, or other traps, all of which lose much of their appeal when we put our faith in Divine Mother rather than the empty promises of Satori's traps. We recognize that Divine Mother is not the ultimate reality, but it is an aspect of DM, and one that holds endless benefits for us along our journey.

Ultimately, none of these concepts or guises can capture or define DM, for DM can only be found in Direct Experience, and that experience can only be had when we are no longer trapped in the Little Me. So don't worry about offending DM by not choosing the right guise. You can use Divine Mother (which I recommend, as it has so many advantages and creates such a wonderful gameplay), God, the laws of physics, or the Flying Spaghetti Monster. DM doesn't mind what you choose. It's just about what works best for you, and what "face" you want DM to have.

What about this idea that we are DM? We might imagine that we exist on a spectrum – on one side, we are firmly entrenched in Little Me, powerless and fearful. On the other side, we are DM, unlimited in every way. Satori is all about moving in the direction of our DM nature, and as we do, we will discover our limits beginning to fall away. But Satori will do all it can to continue programming Little Me, so that Little Me is always calling out: "Over here, look at this shiny new car! This will make you happy! Or this – a chance to make some really good money! Or that person over there – if you can get that person to love you, then you'll finally be happy!"

This idea of becoming DM is confusing, because Little

Me imagines itself in the role of DM, having power over all the things it lusts to have power over in the world. And in a way, this is true for a little while. As we move across the spectrum, closer to our DM nature, there will be a time when we are part Little Me and part something else, and during that time we'll find that through surrender, we can start to shape the world around us, a little like a watered-down version of Cowan. But at some point the Little Me has to transform, and that transformation is much like the transformation of a caterpillar into a butterfly. The caterpillar doesn't just make a cocoon and grow wings. It makes a cocoon and then dissolves into a liquid. And from that liquid a butterfly is formed, the elements coalescing into a new incarnation that is unimaginable from the caterpillar's perspective. Is it the same creature, or something completely different? This gives us a tiny hint of the transformation waiting for us if we solve Satori.

Until then, we inch our way across the spectrum, sometimes moving closer to our DM nature, sometimes being lured back into Little Me. We may have to play Satori many times, forgetting ourselves again and again with little or no memory of ever playing Satori before. But eventually, we will all solve the game. We will all come back to our DM nature, for there is nothing *but* DM.

Cowan Faol Speaks – *Honor your journey. As we hear about DM, we might feel like Satori is hopeless. How can this fragile Little Me ever become something so big, so unknowable, so . . . EVERYTHING? Remember that your Little Me is DM's finest creation, a hiding place so ingeniously crafted that even DM can't find itself without a lot of work. This is one of the main purposes of our Little Me – to be a hiding place and to play the game of finding oneself. And this is also the only way to really, truly enjoy this adventure, because every other route to enjoyment will only be fleeting. Develop your attributes and virtues, avoid traps, and beware the delusion that keeps us ever-lost. Every step closer to your DM nature will bring you into new worlds of enchantment and wonder. Enjoy the ride!*

chapter twenty-three

HELPING OTHERS

As players in Satori, almost all of us long for connection with others. Yet many of us find those connections disrupted by the elements in Satori that push us toward the illusion of separation. Things like social status, appearance, and beliefs will draw lines between ourselves and our family, friends, or those we wish to love. Knowing you are playing Satori (rather than taking it as a hard-and-fast reality) means you will be building your attributes and virtues, and taking those separation-based elements less seriously. And that means that you'll find new connections with people, because you won't be striving to prove your points so often (a known disruptor of good relationships).

Yet being a conscious player in Satori also means that you're seeing through the matrix, and noticing how people around you cause themselves immeasurable pain and problems. Like Cowan said back in Chapter Two, we are *all* magic shapers, actively crafting much of the world we perceive around us in Satori. As we start to understand how this works, we may grow frustrated with others who are, according to our current understanding, invoking the very problems they say they are trying to overcome.

In these situations, we may want to grab someone, shake them, and say: "Dude, you are IT! Stop creating these situations for yourself over and over again! Can't you SEE?"

The truth is that we *can* help others to solve Satori, or at least to make some progress forward. But for you, the act of helping can either be a distraction, or one of the most powerful tools in your arsenal for making your *own* progress in the game. Knowing how to make it the latter is essential.

First we must understand how helping others can be a distraction, pushing us back into level one and the Little Me. This happens when our desire to help comes from our own frustration (frustration being the Little Me wanting the world, or in this case a person, to "look" a certain way). Indeed, when we look at someone and feel frustrated with the way they seem to be sabotaging themselves, it's usually a sign that our Little Me is doing the same thing. We feel the greatest frustrations when we witness others making the same mistakes we're making.

Frustration is the indicator here. If we feel frustrated with someone's lack of progress in the game, we can be sure that we won't be able to help them at all, since our "help" is coming from our Little Me (who has no idea how to do anything but get lost in Satori). But remember compassion? If our desire to help comes from compassion, then we know our help has an actual chance of being helpful.

Still, to help someone along in Satori, we must be very aware of their Little Me. In fact, this is a good thing to remember in all our interactions with other people. Our Little Mes are very delicate. And once they put up their defenses, the person will no longer hear us. Anything that could be construed as an attack will invoke those defenses. The way to avoid those defenses is compassion – coming into the other person's shoes, validating their feelings, and making connection.

Let's see an example. You have a friend who is constantly busy, and often complains about how much they have to do. Over and over again, you watch them make choices that put more load on their shoulders. Plus, from the perspective of knowing the inner workings of Satori, you notice that they are putting all of their extra energy into "solving" their problem through the usual means, by reading books on managing time, spending money on seminars about doing less, and going on meditation retreats. And then they go right back to the same cycles of taking on too much.

Coming from our Little Me perspective, we might approach our friend and say: "Can't you see how you're causing your own problems? You were complaining last week about how much you have on your plate, and then you added the task of helping your neighbor clean their yard this week. How are you ever going to have less of a load if you just keep piling it on?"

Now, everything we said in this example might be true. We might even say it in a tone of voice that doesn't sound too exasperated. But because we approached the issue straight-on, our friend's Little Me has a high chance of going into defensive mode. As soon as it does, the conversation is effectively over, because all of their mental energy will just go toward defending themselves, and they won't hear a word you say. In fact, we can simply remember that when someone starts defending themselves, communication is probably not going to be effective. See defensiveness? Just stop and approach the problem again later on from a different angle.

Coming from our compassion perspective, we might avoid the Little Me going into defense mode by using validation and really stepping into our friend's shoes.

"You know, it must really feel overwhelming sometimes to have so much on your plate. Still, one of the things I admire most about you is that you are always helping people, reaching out to those in need. That's a shining example for us all. Sometimes I wonder if in a weird way, you could help people *more* if you helped people less. Does that make sense? Like, taking on fewer projects, but really applying yourself to the project you're doing?"

In this way, you're giving the Little Me assurance that it's not bad, and in a sneaky way, you're urging your friend to be more immersed and present (which will lead them at least a little step in the direction of solving Satori). If you can get your friend to start a conversation, really confiding in you, then you might get to the point where you can ask them if they see any ways they could transform their situation. And if *they* think of the idea, there will be a much higher chance of them sticking with the solution and making some real progress.

As we journey onward in Satori, remember that it's a great thing if we can help others on their journeys. Especially as we gain in wisdom, and can steer people in directions that will make a real difference in their lives. But we must always be aware of the power of the Little Me – both in ourselves, and in the people we're trying to help. Until we've totally transformed the Little Me, we have to deal with its presence. If we are aware of its tendency to get defensive and then close down all chance of communication or learning, we can watch for that defensiveness and only try to make change when defenses are down.

DM Speaks – *In helping others you help yourself, for you are all you witness around you. Yet the desire to help can also lead us ever-deeper into illusion. Reach out to those around you as if you were helping yourself, for you truly are.*

---

chapter twenty-four

NATURE AS THE ULTIMATE GAMEPLAY

I remember the first time I played *Halo*. My companion and I landed on Installation 04 and looked about ourselves in awe. Nowadays we might look back and see the graphics as outdated, but at the time it was the first moment I truly "lost" myself in a video game world. I was standing there, gazing out over the alien environment, enraptured by the beauty of the scene. Throughout the *Halo* games there were many instances like this, when I'd explore the nature-based areas of the *Halo* world and find them strangely beautiful. Later, immersive games like *The Witcher 3* created even more enthralling natural environments. Many gamers report that they love exploring these forests, mountains, and shorelines during their gaming adventures. In *Eastshade,* you get to explore stunning environments without ever having to fight things (instead, you are a painter painting those gorgeous views).

In Satori, nature also delivers incredible opportunities for gameplay. In fact, nature hands-down offers the most powerful arena for making huge steps forward in the game. I learned this by observing our Forest Monks at ReWild University. Monks take part in an experience that is almost impossible to come by in today's world, leaving technology behind for four months or more and living fully immersed in the natural world. There, they discover how nature is specifically created in the game in order to further our advancement.

Notice that this powerful gameplay environment is made inaccessible to many of us. Unless you are among the exceptional few, you probably don't live in a place where you can step into vast forests outside your back door. Where there are natural areas, they tend to be rule-bound, so that you're not free to go out and live there for an extended period. And many forces within Satori, from movies to plush beds, act to direct your mind toward levels of stimulation or comfort that can make nature seem unpleasant, boring, or even frightening.

If we find ways to break through these barriers, we'll find that wild places deliver a potent alchemy our civilized world can never approach. That's because nature has a magical way of simultaneously calming and nurturing our minds while also providing challenges.

And sometimes those challenges are of soul-crushing levels.

First the nurturing. Studies repeatedly find that nature exposure (and even just having some plants in your room or gazing out a window) has mental and physiological benefits that are in line with advancing in Satori. Think increased focus, less stress, reduced anxiety and depression, and increased short- and long-term memory. You get these benefits just by walking down a path and gazing around yourself.

At the same time, nature exposure can bring challenges. At ReWildU, Forest Monks have to deal with hordes of mosquitoes, encounters with bears, heat, cold, endless days of rain, ground-shaking thunderstorms, ticks, and sometimes hunger or thirst. At times, these challenges can drive Forest Monks almost to the breaking point. Imagine going days without food or sleep during your solo, sitting alone in a deep forest as rain drenches you and lightning flashes dangerously close. As morning dawns, the storm abates, but mosquitoes come at you so thickly that you can hardly breathe without inhaling one. Then the wolves begin howling, their mournful calls echoing through the black-cloaked trees.

Sound scary? You don't have to immerse yourself in nature as deeply as a Forest Monk, because even a short walk through the woods can bring encounters with biting flies, a sudden cold rain, or spine-shivers from something large and unseen crunching through the twilight forest.

Yet as nature explorers face these challenges, they are simultaneously immersed in an environment that automatically provides those mental and physiological benefits we talked about. See how it works? Even as nature breaks you down, it builds you up. And in Satori's gameplay, nature will usually deliver the perfect balance, especially if you enter the forest with an attitude of being open to whatever clues nature will give you.

Our human-built civilization also provides challenges, ranging from minor to soul-crushing. But it doesn't automatically provide those same mental and physiological benefits that nature does. Instead, it replaces nature's nurturing with a constant attempt to provide comfort. Isn't comfort the same as nurture? Not at all. Comfort weakens us, while nurture strengthens us. Comfort *feels* good, but it's actually a distraction that can slowly erode our attributes and virtues. Just think of how a couch lures us in, getting us to sit with crappy posture for hours at a time. Our bodies suffer, and the comfort of that couch might also prevent us from engaging with life in many other ways, creating the proverbial difference between the armchair adventurer and the real-life one. Thus, unless we find specific ways to nurture ourselves, our civilization will break us down with challenges and will try to band-aid those challenges with comforts, but won't actually nourish us or build us up.

If you have access to nature (or can alter your gameplay so that you do), you can log more nature time and you'll automatically gain benefits while clues are delivered by wind, rain, and snow. If you don't have easy access, you can sometimes find nature in surprising places, from a potted plant to the weeds sprouting up through a crack in the pavement to the spider making a web in a dark corner of your closet.

One final benefit of nature. When you're out in the woods or fields, you are surrounded by all sorts of non-human entities – birds and trees, snails and squirrels, butterflies and ants. These entities aren't just decoration in the game. Instead, they are all (in a way our human minds find difficult to conceptualize) 100% lost in the game, and 100% found. They ARE the Core. And one level up from the Core, they are DM. In these non-human entities, DM is fully immersed in being a bird, tree, snail, squirrel, butterfly, or ant, while at the same time still being aware of its own DM nature. We humans, by contrast, can be seen as either special or as the fools in the parade, for we start out at 100% lost, and can only become found through successfully navigating Satori's gameplay.

Thus, when you go out into nature, you are surrounded not by a bunch of mindless "stuff", but by countless Ninja Jedi Zen Masters, some with wings, some with leaves, some with Fibonacci spiraled shells. It's good company, and if we can set aside our fears or discomfort with nature and begin to see all of these entities as our teachers, many doors will open. Of course, we have to learn their "language", which isn't easy. But this non-verbal language is important because it can lead us toward unraveling clues and beginning to enter a participatory world-view in which we get the first glimpses of our unity with DM. In fact, at ReWildU, Forest Monks who spent enough time in nature while also learning meditation and other skills that made them more receptive, would often have spontaneous awakening experiences. One moment they would be sitting on a log, and the next they would glimpse the universe.

All of this is a long way of saying that the more you get outside, the better.

Cowan Faol Speaks – *During my magical training, at a time when I was mastering shape-shifting, I spent a year alone on a small island off the coast. I spent almost the entire time non-human, becoming snails, birds, trees, sharks, worms, and stones. This year was perhaps the most powerful time of transformation for me, allowing me to leave behind limiting human perspectives. You may not yet be capable of shape-shifting, but if you enter nature with a truly receptive attitude, the fully lost-fully found Beings of nature can reveal to you the secret behind this game we're all playing.*

chapter twenty-five
A BIT OF PHYSICS

There is one final concept we must understand if we're to solve Satori. We'll cover it in-depth in Chapter Twenty-Six, but first we have to work on bending our mind's conception of physics a little bit so that this final concept will have a chance of sticking.

In the non-participatory mindset that is given to us when we begin Satori gameplay, we are separate beings living in a largely hostile world of external forces. The world around us acts independently of us, and is local, mechanistic, and deterministic. In other words, it does its own things, and the only way we can affect how things turn out is by directly manipulating the world around us. We do this by moving things around or otherwise interacting with the people/objects around us to try to get them to do what we want.

We can liken this to what you experience when you are, for instance, playing a large open-world game. There is a physics engine that makes sure everything acts as it should when you swing your sword, shoot a gun, drive a vehicle, or ride a horse. You shoot an arrow and it takes some time to hit the target. It doesn't, for instance, teleport there instantly. Confined by the physics of the game, we can become very convinced of the world's behavior. If we try to push over a cart, it will topple. If we try to push over a castle, we'll just do a lot of grunting. If we step off a cliff, it won't be good.

And if we dig deeper? For instance, what if we were programming the game, or the game was so realistic that we had the potential, within our gameplay, to do research and see "behind the scenes" of the game physics? We'd soon find that the physics were just a set of rules imposed on the game, and the reality those physics implied did not equate with the *real* reality our deeper digging revealed.

Let's use an example of shooting that arrow. We pull back the bow and shoot. The arrow travels over an arc, covering an amount of distance that is determined by how far we pulled the bow back, the effects of gravity, and any other forces the game's physics engine imposes. By observing and measuring the different forces involved, I can begin to make some conclusions about the world I'm in. For instance, observing the objects and forces, I can conclude that there is a thing called "distance" or "space" which the arrow must travel through in order to reach its target.

But here's the catch. If we were a programmer, or could otherwise see behind the scenes, we'd recognize that there is no distance in the game. No space. The assumption or illusion of space arises only out of the way that pixels are rendered according to the physics engine of the game.

In Satori, there are two separate ways of seeing physics. In the first, we take the game's physics as the ultimate reality. The physics we observe compel us to draw conclusions about reality which, though they will function very well for almost all applications in the game, are nonetheless only rendered by the game's physics engine. The game's physics may or may not correspond with the deeper physics behind the game, in the "real world". In the second, we somehow see behind the scenes and discover that there is another explanation for the physics we observe in the game, and that there is a deeper, hidden reality behind the apparent one.

The science we've collectively done in Satori is leading us slowly into the second way of seeing physics. Scientists strive to see behind the scenes, and some of what they've discovered, particularly in the realm of quantum physics, suggests that things like space and time and distance may not be as "real" as we've been led to believe. As science progresses in our world, it will continue to unravel clues and continue to discover that the world we're experiencing in our everyday life has something very uncanny operating behind the scenes – a set of rules behind the rules, of physics behind the physics, which point to the "real world" being quite a bit different from the "common sense" world we all experience.

In particular, the most savvy scientists now understand the world to be non-local, meaning that at its most fundamental level, there really is no space or distance as we know it. And they understand the implications of quantum indeterminacy, which suggest that the world exists in a state of information or potential until it is in some way observed, at which point it "collapses" into an observed reality.

If your mind is rebelling against these alternative views of physics, this is a good moment to stop and remember that this book isn't actually about defining reality. As we'll see in the next chapter, it's not so much about how the world actually is, but how we perceive it to be. How it feels. There may not be enough evidence for you to decide whether the world is actually what our "common sense" tells us, or if it is much weirder. But when you choose one way of seeing the world over another, it will have profound effects on your gameplay.

Here's a breakdown of these two ways of imagining the world.

The old "common sense" observations of our world see the world as:

Mechanistic – The world in all its forms is like a big machine, with different parts that operate together to make things run. Many parts (such as you or me) are largely expendable, but all serve to continue the overall operation. The world doesn't "care", have intelligence or consciousness, or otherwise have attributes that you couldn't find in, say, a clock. The world is very "practical". Our mindset or wishful thinking won't change the world. Only hard work or focused effort will.

Local – The parts of the machine interact locally. In other words, for one atom to affect another, they have to bump up against each other. Distance and space are real, and unless we are close enough to something to affect it via some form of bumping (this can mean actually pushing something with your hands, by using sounds such as our voice, using different types of electromagnetic energies, etc.), we have no effect over it.

Deterministic – The world operates by the laws of classical physics, and through observing physics we can make intelligent conclusions about reality. When one thing pushes against another, it will cause an effect, and if we could compute all the interactions, we could understand what was going to happen next in the world. This even includes you – your consciousness is just the squirting of chemicals and firing of neurons in your brain, and there is nothing outside of the world except this bumping together of things and the causes and effects they create.

The new, participatory observations of the world see the world as:

Organic – Instead of a big machine, the world is "mutually arising", as the philosopher Alan Watts put it. A tree doesn't grow by stacking one cell on another like a factory machine, but grows "all of one thing", expanding in all directions as it participates with soil, sun, water, and fungi in a growing process that is interdependent with all the other things in the universe that are also "mutually arising" in unison.

Non-local – Distance and space are not real, but rather only apparent realities. My ability to interact with the world is not wholly limited by space and distance. My state of mind, for instance, may affect the world around me in ways that don't involve atoms or known forces bumping up against each other.

Non-dual – The world is both deterministic and non-deterministic. And neither. Even cause and effect are only illusions which, although they function well in gameplay, don't tell us about the actual world behind the game. We possess the ability to get behind the scenes and participate in the world in ways that might seem very strange to the deterministic mind.

Note that both of these ways of seeing the world are viable. Both are ways of interpreting the data we receive through our senses. Neither is more "correct" than the other. But the way we see the world *does* have a profound effect on our life experience. Satori gives us the "old", non-participatory view as default. To solve Satori, we must begin shifting to the "new", participatory view.

Remember when I mentioned quantum indeterminacy? Well, this discovery of science leads us into the next chapter, where we'll uncover the most important concept introduced in this book. The idea of *rendering*.

Morgan Speaks – *I was told that the game would have totally convincing physics. It would feel completely "real", even though the physics of Satori aren't exactly the same as the physics of our world. Part of that is just how good the Beyul designers are, but part of it is also implanted memories which create assumptions. What I mean is that for Satori gameplay, players' minds are programmed with a feeling that our world is real and normal. Seeing what's going on behind the assumptions is necessary to solve Satori, but not easy. Even most of the "great minds" in the world you're experiencing, the ones writing books and holding PhDs and giving TEDx talks, are still subject to the illusion. They believe it's real. The only way to see behind the scenes is to do less THINKING and more SENSING. Thinking only happens in our minds, showing us only our imaginations. Sensing is actual experience, revealing something our imaginations can never quite grasp. We need to really sense what this world is telling us. That opens up doors to glimpsing the Core behind everything you're experiencing.*

chapter twenty-six

RENDERING

At this point, you're understanding the basics of Satori gameplay, and how the world we experience in Satori seems very real and important, but is actually a role playing game that we're meant to solve. There's been a lot to absorb, and to really grasp it requires a major paradigm shift in how we view and interact with the world. Wouldn't it be nice if there was some overarching concept that could put this all into a neat little package so we could better wrap our minds around it?

Fortunately, there is. It's the concept of *rendering*, and as you start to understand how it works, it will change your entire gameplay experience. We've already tacitly approached rendering from many angles in this book, but now we're giving it a name and making things official.

First, let's take a look at how rendering works in a

video game (and, as we'll see, in a paper-and-dice RPG as well).

As you walk around in a large open-world game, you are quickly immersed in the feeling that the world is expanding all around you. You can see distant mountains, and you know that there is a back to those mountains. You see a nearby ruins, and know that there are rooms to explore inside the ruins.

But there aren't. At least not yet. In order to have enough computational power to create such massive worlds and for us to experience them in 3D, the world isn't actually all there at once. It only exists as models, as information. It is only when you *look* at something in the game that the information (or potential) is *rendered* by your graphics card. In fact, nothing you can't see directly is ever being rendered (this isn't completely true as modern games can pre-render adjoining scenes, but you get the point). You see the front of a person and assume they have a back, but they don't. Their back exists only as a model, as information, until you step behind them and look. It is the act of your character's observation that renders the world around you.

Interestingly, it's much the same in pen-and-paper RPGs as well. You are playing in a world that is vast. Your DM could let you walk for weeks or even months, and you'd find towns and mountains and ruins and seas. But you don't "render" anything in your mind's eye unless you are experiencing it. The rest of the world exists as a vague potential and as memories, but it's not until you step into the ruins, look around, and the DM says that you see an old pirate's chest that the scene is rendered in your mind.

In a video game or a pen-and-paper RPG, when a tree falls in the woods and no one hears it, it doesn't make any sound. In fact, it hasn't even fallen. It exists only as potential until it's observed.

But what about in our world? Does the tree make a sound? Our old, common sense view says it does. The world exists independently of us, and the observer doesn't play a part. But our new view suggests otherwise.

Let's look at some clues from the world we're all experiencing right now. Imagine you're standing on the shore of a lake, looking at the reflection of the sun on the lake's surface. The reflection is bright, almost blinding, and you can point directly at it.

Now, down the shore your friend is looking at the reflection of the sun as well. They point at it, and it's clear that they are pointing to a different location on the lake's surface.

Does this strike you as odd? What if a hundred people were standing along the shore? You are all looking at the same "thing" (the reflection of the sun), yet you're all seeing it at different locations on the lake. And if we added up all the reflections seen, there would be a hundred of them on the lake, at least from the perspective of the viewers. So . . . is there one reflection, or a hundred? Furthermore, what if you were in an airplane and looking down at the lake and the sun's reflection? From that vantage, the entire lake might be glowing brightly. This makes things even more mysterious. From high above (or, if you can imagine, from the viewpoint of a million perspectives standing on the shore at different heights and spacings), the entire lake is glowing. Yet when you look, you see only one small reflection on the lake's surface. In other words, there is a fuller reality (light reflecting off the entire surface of the lake), but you, as a single perspective, render only one sliver of the full reality – the single reflection.

A rainbow is similar. You see it arching from the tree and ending at the big rock. Your friend sees it arching from the barn to the old fallen log. If you had a million people standing there, they'd all see the rainbow in a slightly different place from the person next to them. In fact, the whole sky in front of you is actually refracting light, and the "bow" we perceive is only rendered by our particular perspective. Again, there is a larger potential reality that is invisible to us, and we only render out one sliver of that reality from our particular viewpoint.

And the tree? When it falls, it sends vibrations through the air. These are the information, the potential. If they hit the ears of a human, the expected sound will be rendered out of that information. If they hit the ears of a deaf man, no sound will be rendered. If they hit the ears of a dog or a chickadee or an elephant, sounds will be rendered that our ears are incapable of hearing. In other words, the information interacts with different "graphics cards" and "sounds cards" to create different renders.

This may be true for things like reflected light or sound waves, but what about real, solid things, like trees or cars or people? The truth is that we can never know. Anything that comes into our awareness is in our awareness, and anything outside of it is not currently detectable by us. We might use remote cameras or other devices, but still, we can only see what we are seeing via our own senses (through that device). Everything outside of our awareness? We have no way of knowing whether it is permanently rendered or if we only render things when we observe them.

Oddly, this is unlearning one of the most important skills we learned as infants. It's called "object permanence", and we learned it when we understood that when our parents put a stuffed bear into a box, the bear was still in the box and we could crawl over there and get it out. But that old lesson came with hidden pitfalls, because an object-permanent world leads directly to the idea that we are living in a mechanistic universe. What if, for a moment, we entertain the idea that we may be in a world that is rendered only when we observe it?

Remember that it's not so important what the "truth" of reality is — whether we render things or not. And there is probably no way to determine what is "truth". But the viewpoint we hold powerfully effects our gameplay.

From this new viewpoint, when we look around us, everything is rendered as we view it. Take a look around you. Marvel at the detail of the rendering. Notice how a tiny shift of your head creates changes in the rendering. Realize that you are *co-creating* the world through your observation. You are fully participatory. The world you are experiencing would not exist without your presence. You are taking a larger potential reality and crafting it, through the power of your presence, into a tangible reality that you can interact with.

This is pretty amazing. You are no longer just a bag of flesh squishing your way around a world that exists independently of you. Instead, you have become a *co-creator of reality*. You and the vastness of universal potential (which we might also equate with DM) are dancing together, crafting a reality that can only exist when both of you are working together.

Notice how, as you look around and imagine you are rendering the world, it makes you a more conscious player in Satori.

Realizing we are actively rendering the world means that —

We are participatory in the world. The world doesn't happen TO us. We are actively co-creating the world.

Our awareness increases because we are more actively engaged with the details of our world.

We spend less time feeling like a victim, because we realize we are co-creating our reality.

We become more adventurous and exploratory, becoming curious about how we can participate in the world more fully.

We shift from feeling that we are in conflict with the world (the world is a big thing out to get me) to feeling we are in cooperation with the world.

Even other people become co-creations and co-creators, and we realize that "me" and "other" may not be as separate as we once imagined.

Over time, our understanding evolves of just how the co-creation works, and as it does, we move closer and closer to being able to be almost "magical" in how the co-creation manifests.

We can go really deep with this rendering concept. At first we might just marvel at how the world looks through this new perspective. But eventually, we'll find that all of the things we covered in the book thus far give us tools to co-create a different world, and to see behind the matrix to what is really going on behind the scenes.

Cowan Faol Speaks – *As you begin to grasp that we are actively rendering the world as we observe it, you realize that you are a magic-shaper, as are all the people around you. We are each creating our own reality, much like the people looking at the reflection of the sun on the surface of the lake. There is a shared reality, but simultaneously everyone is creating their own unique version. You will notice that you are all in the shared game-world of Satori, but some people see a world that is dark and despairing, others see a world that is glorious and beautiful, others see a world that is filled with adventure. You are now ready to begin learning how to be conscious of your magic-shaping, and there is nothing quite so fun in life. Will you have the courage and wisdom to learn how to shape your world consciously? If so, what world will you create? And will you be able to see the secret that waits for all of us behind the veil of apparent reality? Great insights await you, my friend. Don't be afraid to go deep.*

chapter twenty-seven

JOURNEY ONWARD

You stand at a crossroads. Now that you understand what Satori is, and how we're all playing a giant RPG (though it is essential to remember that even this idea is a myth), we can be like Cypher in *The Matrix* and decide to stay lost in the game, or we can take the red pill and begin to enter a truer, more exciting reality.

Cypher says that "ignorance is bliss", and believes that if he can lose his memories and be rich and become someone "important, like an actor", then he will be better off. We might feel the same temptation to forget all about Satori and just remain lost in the dramas of life. Cypher forgets that he'll have to spend a lot of time managing his money, or worrying about how the stock market crashed, or, if he's rich enough to hire someone to manage his money, how often he'll be frustrated with that person because they didn't pick the right investment. He's forgetting how being an actor means having to deal with a director you can't stand, or having to shoot a scene over and over again because the camera operator didn't get things right, or how reading a critic calling his acting "lame" is going to make him so angry that he won't be able to sleep for two nights in a row. Because one thing is guaranteed – if we choose to be lost in Satori, it will give us a pretty random mix of good and bad. And in Satori, the goods always comes with hidden bads (and conversely, the bads always come with hidden goods).

On the other hand, if we choose to play Satori consciously, we'll get the same random mix of goods and bads, and sometimes it might seem like we're getting more bads (as we spoke about in Chapter Twenty), but this is only an apparent reality, created because we're paying more attention to the bads and trying to learn from them. For each good or bad that we navigate and transform, we make a step forward on our journey, and move closer and closer to the time when Satori won't need to pepper our lives with this roller-coaster of experiences. Instead, as we move closer to solving Satori, we enter a smoother gameplay where our lessons are more subtle. They may even seem "gentle".

If we choose to journey onward and play Satori consciously, we're in for quite a ride. There will be times you might feel like Cypher, and wish you could go back to being lost. Playing Satori consciously is fun, and can become almost magical, but it's lots of work too, and you might often be frustrated with your lack of progress or with how your Little Me drags you back toward level one.

Here are a few final tips to speed you on your journey.

First, remember the power of stillness and slowness.

Stillness is taking time alone or with someone who is on your journey with you, without any distractions. This might be a walk in the park, or a slow bike ride in the country, or finding a rooftop and staring up at the stars. With stillness often comes insight. Your mind may experience boredom in these moments, but boredom is only the sensation of your mind slowing down and becoming more powerful. Surrender to that sensation, and notice that it's not as painful as you've been led to believe.

Slowness is moving without haste or hurry, especially when people are rushing you. Rebecca says: "Never rush that which must be done quickly." This is a powerful hint, because rushing through a situation guarantees that the Little Me is invoked, and we miss any clues the situation might hold. In addition, it habituates our mind to rushing, until we find ourselves rushing through life in general, and that is the path to becoming ever-more-lost in Satori. Go slowly, and we'll start to immerse ourselves, enter the participatory mindset, and be able to act out of wisdom. Especially when the game tries to overwhelm you with chaos or things to do, go slow.

Second, approach NPCs. They hold endless clues. Often the clues are held by NPCs who are most intimidating to you. Don't be foolish and approach someone who is obviously intent on harm, but do challenge yourself to approach people you don't feel quite comfortable with.

Remember the town of Pahoa in Hawai'i with all the spinners? As we adventure in Satori, we soon see that "normal" people are really spinners, talking to themselves all day long (even if it's silently in their heads), repeating harmful behaviors over and over, and interacting mostly with their head-fantasies rather than the reality that is hiding behind the matrix.

This might be why spinners can make us so uncomfortable, because they reflect a truth we are afraid to admit. That homeless guy might be hitting himself in the face over and over while he mumbles to himself, but that's just an out-in-the-open version of what most of us are doing. For him it's slapping himself in the face, for a "normal" person it might be continually inflicting self-harm through crappy food, bad media, cigarettes, or dramatic relationships. At least the spinner isn't hiding their craziness. And in some ways, an encounter with a spinner may give some immense clues. For instance, unlike most of us who are very concerned about what others think of our Little Me, most spinners have actually advanced beyond that, and from them we can learn to be "ourselves" without fear.

We can learn from every NPC we encounter. Remember they are all there for a purpose, especially when they stand out (for good reasons or bad) in your gameplay. Each NPC is also a PC, and each one is really DM in disguise, and if you treat them that way, clues have a much higher chance of being delivered to you.

Third, remember that in Satori, good things and bad things are essentially the same. This is radical (after all, we would much rather win ten million dollars in the lottery than get a diagnosis of cancer, right?), but true. There are only two paths leading out from every situation. One is to use a situation to help you build your attributes and virtues, reveal clues, and lead you forward. The other is to get caught up in Satori's trap of trying to get you to endlessly manipulate the world. This desire to manipulate the world comes from the Little Me, and it's rigged, because Little Me can never manipulate the world to achieve true joy – it can only achieve temporary, fleeting fixes that don't bring actual satisfaction or fulfillment.

Fourth, don't discount your virtues. It is easier for most of us to think of building up our attributes (who doesn't want to increase their character's attribute scores?), but virtues can seem weak or useless, and often the whole concept is soured by religious preaching we've heard in the past. Remember that if we encounter the world through our Little Me, we'll not only harm those around us, but we'll plunge ourselves deeper into delusion, getting ourselves tangled in level one. Live by our virtues, and we break free of illusion, see our connection with every other element in the game, and unearth clues. The virtues are the literal keys to solving Satori.

Fifth, stay immersed. In level one and two, Satori will throw everything it's got at you to keep you stuck in mind-chatter, fear, and distraction. It will do almost anything to keep you from seeing through the matrix and discovering what is waiting for you. Honing your focus, meditating, and learning to see DM in everything and everyone around you are just a few ways to lead yourself into deeper immersion. Then DM will make your gameplay more fun, and clues will start appearing more often. And stay present. Don't fall for the delusion of thinking the past or future is "real". There is only the moment we're in, an infinite split-second that encompasses the entire scope of the ultimate reality, even including what we call "past" and "future".

Sixth, don't underestimate the power of Satori's distractions. Media is just one example. The people creating media are often better at controlling our focus than we are. They sculpt our opinions, assumptions, judgments, ideas, and motivations. Most people in Satori are complete slaves to this media, while vigorously defending the media's control by insisting that the opinions, assumptions, judgments, ideas, and motivations are really their own. Don't fall for the trap.

Seventh, remember that Satori is an immense open-world game, with a world that extends around the globe, below the seas, and even out into space. Satori will try to convince you that this isn't true, and that you need to stay inside a very little world that has very few choices. But that's just Satori gaming you. Don't buy it. Instead, develop an adventurer's spirit.

Eighth, be honest with yourself. Your Little Me is the world's best liar, and especially likes to convince you that you are transcending the Little Me when all you're really doing is creating new and more subtle versions of the Little Me (that are thus more difficult to transform). Question EVERYTHING the Little Me says.

Ninth, help others. Like in any well-crafted game, if you help people they are much more likely to give you clues or open up doors in the game-world for you. Rebecca and I have made friends around the world through our YouTube channel, which means that if we travel, we have companions wherever we go. But there's a special secret about helping others. If we do it with expectation of return, that's just the Little Me wanting to be rewarded. If you can give without any expectation of return, you tap into your DM nature, for DM gives merely for the joy of giving.

Tenth, practice gratitude. You can use the GLOW meditation from Chapter Fourteen, or any other gratitude practice. Gratitude develops a sense of fulfillment, which frees you of most of Satori's distractions. Gratitude is one of the most powerful tools in your arsenal, and it never runs out of ammo. The more you use it, the more powerful it becomes.

Eleventh, practice awareness without judgment. This is super Zen, and thus not easy to accomplish, but the more you use meditation, immersion, and focus, the more you'll be in command of what your mind is doing and what it's paying attention to. This will free you of many of Satori's influences that push you back toward level one.

Finally, and most important of all, ENGAGE with Satori. When you see an older person struggling to load their groceries into their car, offer to help. Stop to rescue the lost dog on the side of the road. Help someone fix their flat tire, their broken computer, or teach the neighbor kid to code. Talk to people, explore the world, and conquer the fears that hold you back from being an adventurer in Satori.

Satori is the ultimate RPG. There are endless adventures out there waiting for you, all holding priceless clues that lead you toward solving the game and rediscovering your DM nature. Along the way, all the trials and problems of life become transformed, first by seeing them in a different light, and then by the game actually giving you different circumstances.

Enjoy the journey, fellow Satorian. You now know the secret, have taken the red pill, and can see beyond the matrix. The adventure is about to begin.

For more resources and to discover the Becoming Dungeon Master YouTube channel, visit rewildu.com/becomingdungeonmaster

index

A

B

C

D

L

M

N

O

P

R

S

bibliography

Blake, W. *Songs of Innocence and Experience*. New York: Penguin

Chopra, D. and Kafatos, M., 2017. *You Are the Universe*. New York: Harmony

Cole, K.C., 1985. *Sympathetic Vibrations*. New York: William Morrow and Company

Goswami, A., Goswami, M. and Reed, R., 1993. *The Self-Aware Universe*. New York: Putnam

Hagen, S., 1997. *Buddhism Plain and Simple*. New York: Broadway

____., 2003. *Buddhism is Not What You Think*. San Francisco: HarperCollins

Hahn, T., 1975. *The Miracle of Mindfulness*. Boston: Beacon

Hawking, S. and Mlodinow, L., 2010. *The Grand Design*. New York: Bantam

Herman, A., 1991. *A Brief Introduction to Hinduism.* Boulder: Westview

Kelly-Gangi, C., 2006, *Mother Teresa, Her Essential Wisdom.* New York: Fall River

Langer, E., 2009. *Counter Clockwise.* New York, Ballentine

____. 1997. *The Power of Mindful Learning.* New York: Addison-Wesley

Lanza, R. and Berman, B., 2009. *Biocentrism.* Dallas: BenBella

Miller, B., 1986. *The Bhagavad-Gita.* New York: Bantam

Murchie, G., 1978. *The Seven Mysteries of Life.* Boston: Houghton Mifflin

Reps, P., 1957. *Zen Flesh, Zen Bones.* Tokyo: Charles E. Tuttle

Saraswati, S., 1981. *A Systematic Course in the Ancient Tantic Teachings of Yoga and Kriya.* New Delhi: Yoga Publications Trust

Shaw, M. 1988., *The Paradox of Intention,* Atlanta: Scholar's Press

Shearer, A., 1982. *The Yoga Sutras of Patanjali.* New York: Bell Tower

Suzuki, S., 1970. *Zen Mind, Beginner's Mind.* Tokyo: Weatherhill

Tuccillow, D., Zeizel, J., and Pisel, T., 2013. *A Field Guide to Lucid Dreaming.* New York: Workman

Virk, R., 2019. *The Simulated Universe.* Bayview.

Volkman, A., 1960. Thoreau on Man and Nature. New

York: Peter Pauper

Watts, A., 1966. *The Book.* New York: Vintage

____., 1951. *The Wisdom of Insecurity*. New York, Random House

____., 1958. *This is It*. New York: Random House

Wilczek, F., 2015. *A Beautiful Question*. New York: Penguin

Yogananda, P., 1946. *Autobiography of a Yogi*. New York: The Philosophical Library

Zukav, G. 1979. *The Dancing Wu Li Masters,* New York: Bantam

acknowledgments

I want to thank Giles Anderson, who championed the manuscript as my literary agent. Though he wasn't able to find a house for it, he gave me the confidence that it was a worthy project. There are numerous authors who influenced the thought in this book, who I've listed in the bibliography.

Daniel Hill and Brett Harris were immensely helpful as initial test readers, and both of them have also been important parts of my personal spiritual journey. Kai Peterson and Desiree Klein were indispensable as editors. Seriously, they could be pro.

My mother's interest in philosophy and the books on Yoga and Zen that she had on her shelves during my childhood sparked my interest in the esoteric, and my father's love of exploring the intersection of science and philosophy played a powerful role in my ability to explore ideas from different angles.

Thanks also goes to: Andrea Gerasimo, whose yogic wisdom has been both guide and inspiration; Kate , Todd, Emmet, and Aysa Rose, whose presence in my life adds magic every time I see them; Julia Burgess, test reader and fellow spiritual explorer.

And, as with most acknowledgments, this list can never be complete, as every person who has come into my life has shared some bit of wisdom or held a lesson for me, at least when I've been able to listen. Our Forest Monks, especially, often shared ideas and questions that led to the development of this book.

Finally, immense thanks must go to my wife Rebecca for her guidance, friendly challenges, and never-flagging support and love. She is my editor, co-author on many projects, and the true energy and power behind everything I do. I'm just the "face" of much of our work, but all of it is a co-creation. Too, to my two daughters, whose wisdom surprises me every day, and a special thanks to Liliana, who often seems to "channel" DM. For those who have cultivated the ability to listen, and are able to hear the words of a child without judgment, she often speaks a truth that is deeper than any I've yet encountered from any other person in my life.

bio

Kenton Whitman is an author and life adventurer living in Wisconsin, USA. Along with his wife and daughters, he runs ReWild University, a life transformation and nature immersion school that has changed lives around the world. From their Forest Monk program, where people live in the wilderness for up to 11 months, to their ReWild University YouTube channel, they deliver life-changing wisdom in a spirit of love and compassion. You can learn more at rewildu.com, and discover the Becoming Dungeon Master YouTube channel at rewildu.com/becomingdungeonmaster.

Made in the USA
Middletown, DE
05 November 2026

36543427R10139